I first met Roman and Barbara in 1999 du. Ebenezer's Odessa Base. Having lovingly and faithfully raised their own family ... States, they were now obediently, and with great dedication, answering the call of the Lord to minister to His family.

As my wife and I took part in the day-to-day activities of the base and sailings, we sensed in Roman and Barbara the servant hearts of a true mother and father in the Lord. Their commitment and love for the Jewish people and the Ebenezer teams in their care shines through these pages. In sharing so intimately with their readers, they have honestly spelled out the challenges they faced, the hardships, the sacrifices, and the pain of separation from their own family. But through everything, we see the outpouring of God's grace and faithfulness, bringing strength, perseverance, joy, and great blessings.

The ministry of Ebenezer-Operation Exodus is now engaged in helping Jewish people go to Israel from all nations, and I believe these pages bring helpful, encouraging, and honest insight for those considering serving the Lord out on the field in these challenging and significant days.

—Alan R. Field
International Coordinator
Ebenezer-Operation Exodus

One of the most remarkable events in the last fifty years has been the bringing back of Jews from Russia and the Ukraine by Christians. I cannot recall another instance in Jewish history where Christians gave of themselves wholeheartedly and with time, energy, and money to help the Jews return to the Land of Israel.

It was my privilege to be with Gustav Scheller at the birth of Ebenezer. The ministry was born during the first Gulf War in January 1991 in the safe room of the hotel in Jerusalem, where the International Prayer for Israel Conference was being held. It was an extraordinary experience, where people had to wear gas masks during the prayer times and the matters for prayer were written on a board that everyone could see. It was during those days that God spoke to Gustav, and after he had shared what the Lord had said to him with some of us, we confirmed that God had indeed spoken to him. The work of Ebenezer thus was born.

Roman and Barbara Fialkowski have written their own eye-witness testimony of the amazing development of the Ebenezer work. From their own experience they recount the story of God's faithfulness and grace toward the Jewish people.

The great influx of Russian Jews to Israel is a remarkable phenomenon. It is evidence of the trustworthiness of God and His Word. "Hear the word of the Lord, O nations, and declare it in the isles afar off; and say, 'He that scattered Israel will gather him, and keep him, as a shepherd does his flock'" (Jeremiah 31:10.) The Word of God in all its parts is both reliable and relevant. We cannot trust our newspapers and magazines, but we can trust God's Word. It lives and abides forever.

—Lance Lambert
International Author and Bible Teacher
Jerusalem, Israel

It was during Gustav Scheller's attendance at the Institute of Ministry School, Bradenton, Florida, that he received his call and vision to become involved with Israel in the Middle East. Almost immediately after graduation was the beginning of Ebenezer's vast ministry. *Parting the Black Sea* is a prophetic, timely, must-read treatise for every God-loving servant interested in end-times events.

—Dr. Gerald G. Derstine
Chairman of the Board, Gospel Crusade, Inc.
Founder and Director, Israel Affairs, International, etc.
Christian Retreats, MN, FL, NY, Founder
Institute of Ministry, Founder

God is calling His children back to their ancestral homeland, and against all odds, this miracle is happening before our very eyes. Experience the fascinating journey of one couple committed to the prophetic, end-times move of God known as "Aliyah."

—Robert Stearns
Executive Director/Founder Eagles' Wings Ministries
New York

Parting the Black Sea will touch your heart and move your soul. Roman and Barbara share a fascinating story of how their lives were intertwined with Russia, Poland, Ukraine, Brazil, Vietnam—and all involving Israel and the Jewish people. You will see how God literally picked them up, moved them out, and completely changed their destiny. They said it best, "The God who parted the Red Sea to enable the first exodus is the same God who parted the Black Sea to enable our part in the second exodus." We both found their story to be intriguing and heart rending!

—Dr. James M. Hutchens
Brigadier General (US Army, Ret)
President of *The Jerusalem Connection, Inc.* (www.tjci.org)
and wife, Dr. Pat Mercer Hutchens, author, teacher, and practicing artist

Parting the Black Sea is a must-read. This true life story will captivate you and move your heart like none other. It is a story of love. It is a story of sacrifice and courage. It is a story of God's faithfulness to His Word and to His people.

I met Roman and Barbara shortly after their return to the United States. They came to our church one Sunday morning, and after the service, Mom Detweiler introduced me to her beloved foster daughter and son-in-law. In that moment of divine appointment a deep and abiding relationship between us was born. I knew nothing of their lives, but by the Spirit of God I felt a depth of sacrifice I had never felt before. I pulled up chairs, called to my husband to join us, and said, "Tell us your story." We listened in awe as their words tumbled out. They were words filled with God's never-ending love carried deep within the hearts of a humble man and woman who gave all to go and rescue His beloved ones and bring them home—words filled with drama and danger and joy mixed with the pain of a mission ended and the intense struggles of re-entry into American culture.

In that moment I knew a book must be written. The story had to be told. The story is now here. I invite you to enter another world—where a people whose depth of suffering will never fully be known, where God's faithfulness to His Word shines forth ever brightly, and where God uses humble, faithful servants as His own arms of love to return His people home and redeem a people unto Himself. I invite you to experience the heart of God Himself—*Parting the Black Sea.*

—Pastor Anita Malizzi
Hopewell Christian Fellowship
Telford, PA

Parting the Black Sea

Parting the

The Prophetic Fulfillment of a Second Exodus

Black Sea

Roman and Barbara Fialkowski
with Gail Koop

Pleasant Word
A Division of WinePress Group
PW

ISBN 13: 978-1-4141-1475-0
ISBN 10: 1-4141-1475-3
Library of Congress Catalog Card Number: 2009904473

This book is dedicated to the God of Abraham, Isaac, and Jacob. It is also dedicated to all the Olim who made Aliyah from the land of the north to their Promised Land, Israel. Thank you for allowing us to be a part of your journey. We will never forget you.

Shalom

Contents

Acknowledgments

.....*TO THE JEW first* (Romans 1:16) With deep appreciation and profound gratitude, I want to thank God for my best friend, Gail Koop. Gail, *You are the Aaron I prayed for.* Through this whole process you were such an encouragement to me. Thank you for walking beside me every step of the way. The Lord brought you into my life for *such a time as this* and with my whole heart I want to thank you for making this manuscript what it is today. It is a work filled with sensitivity, passion, and sacrifice. Your attention to every detail is valued beyond words. I am so thankful for the times of fellowship, the lunches, and the many cups of coffee that birthed an open and sincere friendship.

With the writing and completion of this book, I have come to realize that most things in God are a process. After seven years of carrying this burden, I have to pinch myself at times to believe that this book is finally completed. Through the highs and lows and depths of discouragement, to the first word ever written and to the last steps of publication, Lord, you were there. You provided for and met every need. I want to give you center stage and thank you with my whole heart for the inspiration to write during a time of deep disappointment and loneliness. It was through the writing of this book that we experienced the restoration we truly needed. Lord, thank you for seeing this work through to completion.

I want to thank my husband, Roman. I love you, Babe, for your strength and courage to *lay it all down*. I am honored to be at your side in this hour. Thank you for the genuine role model you are for our children and for the unconditional love exchanged between all of us.

I want to thank our children Shannon, Roman, and Keith, for their awesome support and generosity of life that gave us release to accomplish this work. Without your hearts to give the go-ahead, there would be no book. Thank you for your sacrifice.

Thank you, Curt and Anita Malizzi, for your faithfulness and dedication to the Body of Christ. Thank you for your love and support that was poured out upon our lives when we needed it most. Anita, the vision for this book was spoken from your heart into mine, and I am humbled and deeply grateful for the encouragement and the steady flow of confidence you gave to me.

To my "Mom Detweiler," I will never be able to put into words all that my heart holds for you. You modeled a life before me that was steeped in humility, kindness and love. Through your gentle and quiet spirit I came to know Jesus in a real and living way. I am honored to be called your foster daughter and am deeply grateful for the rich heritage you imparted into my life. *I miss you so much.*

Thank you to my foster sister, Judy Moyer, who believed in this work when it was in seed form. Thank you from the bottom of our hearts for your abundant financial provision that enabled this book to be published. May the God of Israel bless you and your generations to come.

Thank you, Dan Reiter, for your profound love and years of nurturing at Community Christian Fellowship. As a spiritual father you wore the garments of compassion, humility, and gentleness that made God's love alive and real to us. We are so grateful to you for imparting into our lives a firm foundation of faith and trust in God which enabled us to meet every challenge.

Thank you to all the Ebenezer volunteers who unselfishly gave of themselves in the work of Aliyah.

Finally, I want to thank all the prayer warriors for their prayers, especially all those who pray for Israel every day and all those behind the scenes who continually asked about the progress of this book and gave a word in season when it was badly needed. Thank you for your love and support. God bless you.

"Thus speaks the Lord God of Israel, saying: 'Write in a book for yourself all the words that I have spoken to you. For behold, the days are coming…that I will bring back from captivity My people Israel and Judah…And I will cause them to return to the land that I gave to their fathers, and they shall possess it.'"

—Jeremiah 30:2, 3

Prologue

THEY WERE LIKE human mules. The ragtag team of men hoisted twenty-four thousand pounds of luggage, bag by eighty-pound bag, onto their backs and up the gangplank of the ship destined for Haifa, Israel. Held together with tape, rope, and belts, the luggage mirrored the lives of the bedraggled souls who had packed them. It was as if these stalwart volunteers from around the world hunched not only under the physical weight they carried but also under the decades of oppression it represented.

The December snow transformed the Odessa port into a treacherous kaleidoscope of white. As the Black Sea conjured a biting wind, the men gingerly mounted the slushy steps. Their eyes, barely visible between scarves and fur-trimmed hats, bulged from the Herculean strain. "Oopa!" "Ach!" "Umph!"

As if mocking them, a perfectly good escalator stood idle next to the makeshift stairs. The Ukrainian guards took joy in creating this final roadblock in returning the "Olim," the Hebrew term for Jews, to their homeland. The hammer and sickle still cleaved to their hearts; the men sneered, saying the escalator would not endure the weight.

Once the luggage was on board, it was the women's job to see that the bags were delivered to the proper cabins. It took two of us, stopping to rest a few times, to deliver one bag. The corridors seemed narrower than the width of the suitcases, which banged against our knees and legs as we made our way to the rooms.

By the end of the day, my palms blistered, my legs were black and blue, and I felt like I had played in a football game. The welts and bruises from the last sailing that had just begun to heal on my husband, Roman's, back were once again raw. I longed for our bathroom back in the States, the never-ending supply of hot water. But hot water, like many of the amenities we took for granted at home, was a luxury in Ukraine. It was only available twice a week, so we'd have to wait two days to take a lukewarm shower at the base.

This was just one of fifty sailings Roman and I helped launch during our two years in Ukraine. The physical, emotional, and spiritual strength necessary to enable each one was absolutely divinely inspired. It never ceased to amaze me how the Lord did this—how He brought Roman and me thousands of miles from home, took us away from our own children to seek His out, and prophetically brought them to their promised land. Called from the corners of the earth, we were a bunch of ordinary nobodies. But together we became God's hands, feet, and heart. In the end, the aching bones, the dire homesickness, and the primitive living conditions didn't matter. We were privileged and grateful to be in the midst of this—actually walking and breathing the Scriptures.

When our time in Ukraine was up, we had seen 16,000 Olim return to Israel. We had helped these people, many of them sick and elderly, to move from darkness into light. Through the grace and faithfulness of God, we had given them something they had lost long ago—that internal sunrise—hope.

But the mission field is a battlefield. The scars it left required a walk through my own personal wilderness before they could heal. So it has taken many years to tell this story. Like a Faberge egg, I have held it close to my heart, afraid that the telling might shatter its significance, afraid that no one would understand. It was so unbelievable that even Roman and I do double-takes whenever we look back.

But now, for many reasons, it is time for this story to be shared. One reason is that my children and their children need to understand why we left them, and why and how this work eventually overshadowed everything, even them. I've tried to explain it, but I always fall short.

Another reason this story needs to be told is that the world needs to understand "Aliyah." Fulfilling scores of Old Testament prophecies, this re-gathering of the Jewish people to Israel continues to unfold as a historic miracle. This book attempts to describe the grass-roots efforts that undergird this prophetic work.

Lastly, and maybe most importantly, it is time for this story to be told because it proves the timeless promise of the Scriptures. It proves, time and again, that God "is the same yesterday, today and forever" (Hebrews 13:8). And through the hearts that were changed after hearing the prophetic words of Isaiah, Jeremiah, and Zechariah, this story shows the keeping power of God's Word, proving that "it shall not return to Me void, But it shall accomplish what I please, And it shall prosper in the thing for which I sent it" (Isaiah 55:11).

Why we were chosen to do this holy work is a question as wide as the wind. Just as Felix and Oscar were The Odd Couple, Roman and I were The Ordinary Couple. Whenever I speak about our work overseas, people ask how we came into it and how we were able to leave everything, even our children, to do it. So I have attempted in the first part of this book to describe who we were before the Lord called us, and how, over the course of the unlikeliest of lifetimes, He drew us into a universe beyond anything we ever could have asked or imagined (Ephesians 3:20)—a universe that so transformed my vision, it's as if I've been given an anointed pair of binoculars. I can now direct my gaze to any point in my life, focus in, and see God—the God of Israel—in all the details.

Chapter 1 ∿

Who We Were

"For I know the thoughts that I think toward you," says the Lord, "thoughts of peace and not of evil, to give you a future and a hope."
—Jeremiah 29:11

FROM A DISTANCE, even the most complicated jigsaw appears seamless. But up close, you can see how each part interlocks, how they come together to create that picture on the box. Roman and I met in 1969, but it would be decades before our picture would come together. Yet, in each other we found the pieces to anchor and create the frame—the pieces of our hearts that had been lost when we were catapulted to adulthood.

I was one of five children. Our family burrowed like moles into the lowest of low-income city housing, changing apartments the way most people change their socks. I still don't understand, especially through the haze they operated in, how the tenants always knew the precise day and time the welfare checks would come. No matter where we lived, the scenario was always the same. As if in a communal sixth sense, people would gather around the mailboxes. In a party-like atmosphere, they'd smoke and shuffle on a carpet of butts, while waiting for the mailman as if he were the Messiah.

My father had his spot, propped against the front doorframe in the lobby. His hands trembled as he chain lit homemade cigarettes, his pants barely cooperating with the makeshift belt tied around his withering frame. His shirt was the one he'd slept in. On those days, I worried about getting the dollar I needed for my bus pass. School was fifteen long blocks away, and it seemed like I was the only kid who had to walk so often. My mom would always argue with my father for the money before he got a chance to blow the whole check on booze and tobacco. I think that's why she started sending me to the country in the summers through the Fresh Air Fund—so she could get me away from that environment.

The year I turned ten, after five summers as a "Fresh Air Kid," I stayed with a family in Pennsylvania, the Detweilers. They were unlike any of the other families I had been sent to. There was no smoking, drinking, or abusive behavior. There was always plenty of food—no one said anything if you took an extra portion or asked for seconds. And Mrs. Detweiler was different from any of the other moms. She gave me hugs all the time, ignoring the turtle shell of protection I had grown. Based on our mutual requests, the Detweilers became my permanent summertime family. It wasn't until twenty years later that I figured out what was so different about Mom Detweiler. It was that she always had acknowledged the Lord. She brought Him into conversations and thanked Him before meals. She and her family became the blueprint for the way I wanted to live. And in large part, I owe my faith to her. She has always been my "mom."

When I was fourteen, my mother died of uterine cancer. Whether my father couldn't take care of us or chose the bottle over us, I'm not sure. But my brother, three sisters, and I were separated and placed in foster homes. The Detweilers weren't an option for me because they only had been a summertime family. But had it not been for Mom Detweiler, the darkness surely would have won.

For the next four years, I was bounced from home to home, with an occasional stay in a boarding school. Unfortunately, the horrors you hear about those places are all true. But through every change and shift in homes, Mom Detweiler kept in touch, tracking me through the foster agency I had been registered with. She sent me letters, cards, and packages for Christmas and birthdays. In response, I'd write thank-you notes back to her. Whenever I'd get a little extra money, I'd call her.

2

Roman's father was a Polish prisoner of war from 1939–1945. In 1944, his mother and her family were taken from Ukraine, separated, and placed in German labor camps. After the war, the labor camps became refugee camps, and that is where Roman's parents met, married, and had three children. They lived in these camps until they immigrated to the U.S. in 1951. Again, looking through those anointed binoculars, I can see the God of Israel watching over Roman's life. At five years old, he came to this country on a ship with hundreds of other immigrants, sailing from a land of oppression and persecution to a land of freedom and opportunity. Only the Lord knew that five decades later Roman would again be accompanying a shipload of immigrants, again sailing from darkness into light.

Like mine, Roman's father was an alcoholic. But he was also abusive. When Roman's mother finally walked out, his father told him that he wouldn't be able to keep the family together unless Roman dropped out of school and got a job. He was only sixteen. His father's income as a carpenter was minimal, but it was his drinking that continued to threaten their finances. So after finishing tenth grade, Roman quit school and got a job in a local dress factory.

Roman worked five and half days a week on a schedule that would impress even today's corporate efficiency experts. Up at six in the morning, he made breakfast, packed lunches, and got his two younger brothers to the bus. After that, he drove to work, where he had to punch the clock by eight. On the way home, he stopped at the general store to pick up whatever they were running short on. In the evenings, he helped with homework and made sure the boys had dinner and were washed and in bed before nine. On weekends, Roman worked Saturday mornings. The rest of the time, he washed clothes, cleaned the house, and looked after his brothers.

Roman took care of his family this way for two years. When his father remarried, Roman enlisted in the marines. He served in Vietnam for a year, then studied for and earned his GED.

Roman and I were married in 1970, just a year after we met. As I made my way down the aisle, I thought of my mother, missing her more at that moment than at any other time since her death. And I realized that I hadn't really grieved for her before. I don't think I knew how. It was as if I had been protected from feelings that would have destroyed me and kept me from this moment. But as I approached Roman and saw the mix of loss and longing mirrored in his face, I knew that it was okay now. It was okay for two throwaway kids to abandon their armor and begin to heal the tender spots that for so long had needed attention.

In hindsight, our wedding song seems as perfectly orchestrated as the puzzle that began to take shape as we danced our first dance as husband and wife. It was indeed "A Time for Us." It was a time of mending the past and weaving it into the future—a future so skillfully woven into our hearts that its tapestry required decades to complete. And at its center was the Weaver Himself—the One whose passion became our passion, whose vision from the beginning of time became our vision, and who made a single seed sprout in two hearts.

Chapter 2 ⤵

Who We Became

Come to me, all you who labor and are heavy laden, and I will give you rest. Take My yoke upon you and learn from Me, for I am gentle and lowly in heart, and you will find rest for your souls. For My yoke is easy and My burden is light.

—Matthew 11:28–30

1971–1981

IT SEEMS ODD to be able to summarize a decade of marriage in a few paragraphs. But, like I said before, we were The Ordinary Couple.

By 1980, we had three children: Shannon, Roman Eric, and Keith. In 1976, we bought the house in Riverhead, New York, where we still live today. Our children went to the same schools we did and attended The Congregational Church where we were married.

Roman was a tractor trailer driver and spent weeks at a time on the road between New York and the Midwest. I took care of the house, raised the kids, and worked part time at a nursing home in Riverhead. Though we struggled financially, there was always food on the table and clean clothes on our backs. If there was anything at all extraordinary about our family, it was that we leaned on and adored each other. Our house rested on a foundation of laugher and love. And it was love, an eye and heart-opening love, which began steadily to tug on the shirtsleeves of our hearts.

In 1979, our church started to sponsor weekend retreats for married couples. They were called "Marriage Encounters." Initiated by the Catholic Church, these were efforts to draw couples closer to God by focusing on specific Scripture passages about husbands, wives, and families. At one of these retreats, Roman and I were surprised to discover that God was actually interested in us and our marriage.

There was a period during the weekend called "the 90/90," where Roman and I had to separate and sit and write for ninety minutes about why we wanted to go on living with each other. Then we came together to share what we'd written. By Sunday night, a bond had formed between us that hadn't been there two days before. It was as if a third person had been added to our relationship—as if we had been connected to one of those old-fashioned party lines. But our party line had God on the other end.

Over the next two years, that third voice became louder and louder, until neither of us could deny what we were hearing.

About a year later, on a blustery November afternoon, I turned on the TV. *The 700 Club* was on. The sight of Pat Robertson's face and the sound of his voice elicited memories that reeled me in like a fish. Suddenly I was back in Pennsylvania with Mom Detweiler. She had watched that show, a Christian-based news/magazine program, all the time. It would be on as I passed through the living room, but I never paid any attention to it. Wanting to hold on to the warmth that was radiating inside of me, I sat down and listened intently.

Mr. Robertson was talking about Jesus Christ. He said that if I asked Jesus into my heart He would give me peace unlike any I'd ever known and that He would heal every hurt and bad thing that had ever happened to me. All I had to do was ask.

Since being married to Roman, I had developed a sense of peace. I felt safe and secure. I had created a home and a family like I had seen at the Detweilers'. It was something I'd always wanted. But deep down, in those secret places, I was still that throwaway girl, bruises fresh, sensitive to the touch. Ever since that first day at the Detweilers', I had longed for the peace I found in Mom Detweiler's arms. When they were around me, everything else fell away. But the world would always reopen the hollows inside.

As Pat Robertson spoke, I wondered if this could be what Mom Detweiler had—Jesus, the Lord. *Was this where her peace came from? Is this what she tried to give to me, but what I could never hold on to?* If so, then I wanted it. I had wanted it since the first time I entered her house. And as if I were eavesdropping on that party line, I heard a familiar voice telling me, *"This is the way; walk in it"* (Isaiah 30:21).

I watched, awestruck by what was being said. And, like a child, I imagined Mom Detweiler's heart. Through its door I saw Jesus, like a gentle physician, infusing arteries and veins with elixirs of love, peace, and kindness. And right there in my living room, as naturally as if I were inviting Him to dinner, I asked Jesus to come into my heart, too. And in that moment, like a speaker with the bass turned all the way up, my insides resonated with a whole new kind of longing. It was as if all the old canyons had been filled and new ones had opened. I had been "born again," and now I longed to find out more about the One who had just transfused my heart.

Within days I found myself at a Christian bookstore. I was overwhelmed by the choices of Bibles—hard cover, soft cover, full-sized, pocket-sized, standard, and study Bibles. Thankfully, my selection was determined by what I could afford. I wound up with a New Testament, which I read cover to cover in three days.

When I told Mom Detweiler about what had happened, she sent me cassettes of Christian music and sermons by various pastors. I'd listen to the tapes on my walkman as I did my three miles around the high school track. I listened as I prepared dinner or cleaned the house. When I finished the tapes Mom sent, I bought more. I wore out three cassette decks that year.

Even though I never had been interested in history before, I became captivated by the story of Jesus—by *His*-tory. In book after book, Bible story after Bible story, sermon after sermon, the message was the same.

Jesus was the Son of God. He died as a sacrifice so that we could live in right relationship with God the Father. Jesus loves us no matter what. He was real and is real. I believed that "He is the image of the invisible God" (Colossians 1:15). And He became real to me, a real person living inside of me.

I came to understand that the Bible is God's Word, not just some storybook shoved in hotel night stands. And knowing this, each time I read it, the words, the stories, and the people became more powerful, more real than anything I'd ever experienced. I don't know how to explain it other than to say that reading the Word of God became the most thrilling experience of my life. It still takes my breath away.

And as all that I hadn't known continued to be revealed to me, as I began applying what I was learning, my vision became sharper and my mind clearer. I was more joyful, more serene, more grounded. I knew that I was never alone and had never been alone. Even though for many years I had felt like a castaway, I began to feel as if I now functioned on a different level from everyone else. Not better, but different, as if I'd developed a sixth sense. It was like having an invisible safety net wrapped around me.

Roman quietly watched, observing fundamental changes in my character. What I didn't know, but suspected, was that he was looking at me the way I had looked at Mom Detweiler. And the voice on the party line eventually became clear to Roman, too.

The following November, at a Full Gospel Business Men's Fellowship International dinner, the organization's pastor gave the invitation to receive the Lord. My instincts told me what Roman was about to do, so I excused myself and went to the ladies' room. I wanted Roman to do this alone, and I felt as if that's how he wanted it. When I returned, he told me that the pastor had prayed with him. At that moment we embraced in a way that felt like the first time. It was as if we had been given a second chance, a new "Time for Us."

That night, more than ever before, in a way more real than ever before, there were three of us. But it was no longer a party line. It was a lifeline that we would cling to day after day, year after year, as it pulled our hearts towards a tiny country on the other side of the world.

Chapter 3 ❧

Building
a Foundation
of Faith

Therefore whoever hears these sayings of Mine, and does them, I will liken him to a wise man who built his house on the rock: and the rain descended, the floods came, and the winds blew and beat on that house; and it did not fall, for it was founded on the rock.
—Matthew 7:24–25

1982–1992

HAVING FAITH IS trusting in something you can't see. It's like when you were a child and closed your eyes and fell backward into a friend's arms. When I pull out those anointed binoculars and focus in on these ten years, I see how the Lord prepared us to trust Him and gave us what we needed early on so that we'd be able to let Him catch us at the end.

In 1982, Roman landed a local job at Grumman Aerospace. After spending years on the road and being gone for weeks at a time, he was home every night and weekend. I found a part-time job at a doctor's office in Mattituck, where the hours were tailor made for the kids. While working, I met a new group of friends who belonged to Community Christian Fellowship church, which was near the office. Roman, the kids, and I began to attend this church. They took us in like family. It was there that we were introduced to the Christian Family Conferences in Virginia (week-long seminars held in the summer). It was at these conferences that Roman and I first learned that there were Christians concerned with Israel.

Those weeks in Virginia were vacations for us. The kids looked forward to reuniting with friends they'd met and to making new ones. All their activities were linked to Bible studies, and they always brought something they made home. One year Shannon made a beautiful shelf with a Scripture verse painted over it. Roman Eric made an unusual banner out of burlap that had Scripture written at the bottom. Keith made a red Play-Doh heart, showing how our hearts can be softened by the Lord.

Looking back, I see how these years were foundational for our family. Our children were nurtured in the knowledge of the Lord that would allow them to release us, years later, for the work we would be called to do. And it was at these conferences that our own hearts began to be molded and shaped, just like that Play-Doh heart of Keith's.

Lance Lambert, a Bible scholar and teacher from Israel, was the usual guest speaker at the conference. This was the first time I had heard about the Lord's commitment to Israel from a Christian perspective. He spoke of how it was our responsibility as a church to be informed of what we were called to be and do as the younger brother to Israel—to have a love for Israel and be involved in her safety through prayer and support. He also talked about how the Lord wanted to arouse His church to action.

In the early days of our marriage, Roman used to kid around and say that he was going to go to Israel and volunteer for the Israeli Defense Force. He'd returned from Vietnam with an ear tuned to the Middle East. He was fascinated by Israel's ability to survive, their intelligence network, and their soldiers' expertise. He bought books on Israel about the Jewish people, their fight for their land, and their will to survive. It seemed he was always bringing this Little-Engine-That-Could nation into conversations. Now, at these conferences, Roman's ears were pricked like a dog's at attention.

When we were at home, we poured ourselves into our children. There was baseball, football, basketball, track, boy scouts, and girl scouts. We taught Sunday school and took the youth group on weekend retreats.

These were cornerstone years, when the kids became old enough to find that lifeline for themselves, and when they began to hold on, too. And it was during this time that the Lord grounded our marriage, much the same way a three-pronged outlet prevents short-circuiting.

Since Roman and I had been married, any contact with my family had been minimal. Our past begged to be forgotten, and seeing each other only called it back. But soon after my younger sister, Margie, was married, she began to visit. It was one of those visits that pivoted our relationship.

One Saturday when Margie and her little boy, Kelly, were staying for the weekend she said, "Barbara, I want what you and Roman have." Without asking, I knew what she meant. I remembered how I wanted what Mom Detweiler had, how Roman wanted what I had—that Play-Doh heart.

But how could I explain it, this surrendering to what most of the world denies? I didn't feel able. However, as I began sharing with her, telling her what happened to Roman and me, I started to feel more confident. It was the weirdest thing, as if God, through His Holy Spirit, was actually telling me what to say.

But Margie had trouble believing that anyone could love her that much. She was just three when our mother died, and there had been no Mom Detweiler in her life. Neither of us ever really had a father. But I was trying to explain to her that now I did. And all I could do was reassure her that she could too. As she listened, I could see that she was rising up from the same caverns that had trapped me for so long.

The next morning, when the pastor gave the call for salvation, Margie accepted the Lord. Afterward, I gathered some of the women together and we prayed for Margie and her family. What we didn't know was that a short time later Margie would develop breast cancer. She was just twenty-seven, with a two-year-old son. It was as if history was repeating itself, since Margie had been three when our mother died from cancer.

Margie's mastectomy sparked a brief reunion with my brother, John, and sister Linda. John was gentlemanly but removed. Linda was distracted, worried over her son, Jonathan, who was heading for Iraq.

Shortly after Margie's surgery, over a period of about six months, I began to lose the strength in my left arm. After seeing a specialist, we found I had two compressed disks in my neck. Two weeks before Christmas in 1990, I had to have spinal surgery to replace my fifth and sixth disks. I was unable to work for more than a year.

The following year, in November of 1991, we got the awful news that my nephew, Jonathan, had been killed in a motorcycle accident while he was home on leave.

Five months after Jonathan's funeral, in May of 1992, Roman came home early from work. He pulled into the driveway, got out of the car, lifted the hood, and just stood there looking over the engine. It was after three, so the kids were home. They'd heard the car pull in and ran to the kitchen window, excited. "Hey, Dad's home! What's he doing, Mom?" I told them that he probably had some car trouble, though I knew better.

We had prayed about the layoffs that were happening at Grumman. But when I met him on the driveway, Roman told me what I had dreaded. I went back into the house, knowing Roman needed this time to himself. He never lost it, never got angry. He just continued to bend over the engine, arms splayed on the fenders, as if somewhere beneath that hood were all the answers. I knew that the Lord had hold of Roman's heart and would help him find them.

For the next year, Roman was on unemployment and I still wasn't able to work. We had three kids, a mortgage, and the usual household bills. Looking back even now, it seems that has been the Lord's way with our lives. Though our family has received abundant blessings, money has never been one of them.

Encouraged by the Department of Labor, Roman attended electronics school for forty weeks. During that time, Margie's cancer unpacked its terrible valise again. This time, she was terminal.

After Roman's classes, he stopped off at the hospital to visit Margie. For months she looked forward to his visits, when he'd sit by her bed and read to her from his Bible.

On my last visit with my sister, just before Christmas 1992, I prayed for the Lord to take her home. And within two days, He did. Why He answered that prayer and not the one for her recovery is something I'll never know—nor why our prayers for Jonathan's safety and for us to find work hadn't been answered.

As 1993 approached, we walked away from these years that had been so full of promise at the outset, dug in our heels, and fell backward into the arms of the Lord.

Chapter 4 ❧

The Call

For you shall go to all to whom I send you, and whatever I command you, you shall speak. Do not be afraid of their faces, for I am with you to deliver you.

—Jeremiah 1:7–8

1993–1998

WHAT HAD ONCE energized us—church, each other, the kids, and their activities—barely ignited a spark. We were going through the motions, but we were like spiritual zombies. It was as if our faith had moved to our peripheral vision, fogged by the losses of the previous years. But after a time, the Lord once again became the center and focus of our lives.

I had never done anything like it before—gone away with just the ladies, without Roman or the kids. It was the fall of 1995, and I headed off to North Carolina to attend a Christian women's conference. Five of us from the church made the twelve-hour drive. The camaraderie was what I'd always imagined college life would have been like—full of discussion and music and belly-aching, bladder-bursting laughter.

The worship leader for the conference was Robert Stearns, a minister from New York and the founder of Eagles' Wings Ministries. He was charismatic and on fire for Israel. During the course of the week there were several guest speakers, all of whom threaded Robert's stated vision into their speeches. His vision stated that we, as Christians, had a responsibility towards Israel and the Jewish people. He said that we should pray over the biblical prophecy of the return of God's people to their homeland, and we should stand united. I had heard some of this a few years before at the conferences in Virginia. But this time my heart was at attention. And as I listened, I thought of Roman and those early years of our marriage and how he was so drawn to Israel and the Middle East. I thought about how it seemed the Lord had opened his heart in a trench in Vietnam, and how now, twenty years later, He seemed to be doing the same with mine.

During one of the times of worship, a few women began to dance in the aisles. It was something I'd never seen before. Their bodies flowed like water, smoothly bending, twisting, and turning, their arms and hands graceful as a ballerina's. It looked strange, but authentic. And in that room, I felt a tenderness and sweetness I'd never felt before, as if the Lord were dancing right through these women. And like a kid in a candy store, I wanted everything I saw. I wanted to join them. But my inhibitions got the better of me, and I didn't. I just stood there with my eyes closed and my hands folded, letting it all wash over me.

On the third day of the conference, something called a "Watch of the Lord," or a "Night Watch" was scheduled. It was an all-night prayer and worship session, starting right after dinner and scheduled to last until six the next morning. I'd never done anything like this and decided to go.

The wall that divided the two grand ballrooms had been folded back to make a room that seemed the size of a football field. I think all 700 women who attended the conference were there. The mammoth crystal chandeliers that were centered over each room were dimmed. Pillows framed the walls for anyone who might want to rest during the night. Anointed worship music drifted softly through the sound system.

Twice during the night, we had times of communal worship that lasted about two hours. The rest of the time, each woman was left on her own. I had never seen so many people express themselves in so many different ways. Some were on the floor, some were dancing. Others, like me, were on their knees. At one point, as I knelt in prayer, there was a quickening in my spirit. I felt as if the Lord had "knighted" me for something, but I didn't know for what.

That night, I finally lost my inhibitions and danced with the other women. I don't know how to describe how this felt, other than that my body seemed to be separated from my mind, interpreting its love and need for the Lord all on its own. I know it sounds strange to people who can't imagine it. And I expect some will laugh. But I can tell you that it was the most freeing experience I've ever had, as if my very soul became liberated, offered up to God to use and shape.

I felt like I had stumbled upon some hidden, radical movement of God—as if the Lord, called "the Lion of the Tribe of Judah" (Revelation 5:5), was right in that room, shaking his mane, releasing His power, and drawing us closer. And I realized that in all my years as a Christian I had been spiritually standing on only one leg. I understood that there was a whole other dimension to my faith—its Jewish roots. It was as if all those years of Lance Lambert's teaching at the Virginia conferences suddenly became abundantly clear. After fifteen years of scratching the surface, I had just broken ground. And that night, the lassitude that had gripped me for the past two years transformed into a hunger to dig deeper into this revelation given by a God who would continue to astound me.

The women I traveled with were similarly affected by the conference, especially by their new understanding of the church's role with respect to Israel. So we began to hold night watches in our own little church on Fridays after dinner. I brought a cassette player with worship music, just like they played in North Carolina. There were many times we'd spend hours just praying over that nation. We'd open a map on the floor, lay our hands on the city of Jerusalem, and pray for the Lord's people. At the end of the watch, just as dawn was breaking over the field, we took communion. It was a beautiful, special time, as if God were offering up the sun in His fiery palms. We held these watches for about three years.

During this period of time, Roman and I began subscribing to newsletters from Christian ministries in Israel. Friends passed along literature on Israel. Headlines began to grab our attention. Magazine articles that would have previously gone unnoticed caught our eye. It was as if the Lord was making a trail for us. And Roman and I, like Hansel and Gretel, were following the crumbs.

The elders in our church asked Roman if he would share with the fellowship what we'd been learning about Israel. He was honored to have been asked, but nervous, afraid that he wouldn't be a good speaker. He took days to prepare. And when he first started to speak, I could see the insecurity on his face. But as he went on, he relaxed, and I could see the Lord settling him down. I felt the burn of tears as I thought about how the Lord had brought our hearts together like this—how Roman had had a heart for Israel for the past twenty years, and now, so did I. It made me think about what Scripture says about the Lord's timing. "With the Lord one day is as a thousand years, and a thousand years as one day" (2 Peter 3:8).

We visited messianic congregations and went to Seders. As we watched and listened, we began to meet more and more people, Christians and Jews, who carried this burden for Israel, this understanding of God's heart for reconciliation between Jews and Gentiles. Through this network, we found out about a community outreach in Bensonhurst, Brooklyn. It was the summer of 1997, and several churches and messianic congregations had come together to try to show this Jewish community who their Messiah is. There were speakers, a procession with banners, and people handing out literature. Roman and I were thrilled to be a part of this and then taken aback by what we found.

Many people from the community looked repugnant. Rabbis hurled insults and danced and flailed around, trying to make a distraction. One man called us "Jew killers" and showed the numbers on his arm from the concentration camp. When I accidentally brushed up against a rabbi, he pushed me back with a look of disgust and a force that frightened me. I didn't know that it was considered a sin for a woman to touch an orthodox rabbi. But this experience would be something I'd tap into years later, during our work overseas.

Shortly after this outreach, Roman and I attended a conference where a woman led a workshop on the gifts of the Holy Spirit. It was held in a church that was filled so that there seemed to be standing room only. But we found two seats way in the back and settled in, comfortable with being lost in the crowd. The woman, her commanding voice belying her petite frame, walked up and down the aisles, calling people out from the audience. She said that the Holy Spirit wanted to share something with them.

As she moved toward the back of the sanctuary, my eye caught hers. The next thing I knew, she called Roman out of his seat and to the front of the sanctuary. Stunned, he went forward. She asked his name and if the lady sitting next to him was his wife. He nodded, and then she called me out too. My knees were shaking. I could hardly make it to the front. She told us to stand to the side of her and wait, because she didn't yet know what the Lord wanted to say to us. But she knew she was being given something and that the Holy Spirit would eventually speak.

We were self-conscious, silently praying to the Lord to return us to our seats. Then she stood right before us. "I know what the Lord wants to say to both of you." We had never been singled out for anything. My heart fluttered like a caged bird. "The Lord has spoken to me, and the word for both of you is 'Israel.'"

The woman laid her hand on Roman's chest and began to prophesy over him about the burden of the Lord's heart for Israel. Within a few seconds, Roman fell backward, and someone caught him from behind. They laid him on the floor. He was very still, his eyes closed. Next, she placed her hand on my head and spoke of how I was going to be Roman's helpmate. She talked about how the Lord would use us to speak to many of his sons and daughters and many who are veiled in their hearts. She said that the Lord would use us mightily in the days ahead. The next thing I knew, I was lying on the floor. My eyes were closed, I couldn't speak, and the embarrassment and inhibition I'd felt just seconds before were gone. I was completely at peace. When we finally came to our feet, it felt as if we had been in another realm.

This had never happened to us before. It was the first real confirmation that what we had been thinking and feeling about Israel all these years was truly from God. We hadn't just somehow stumbled across a cause that we needed to fill our lives with. Out of a room of hundreds of people, we had been singled out and given this message. What are the odds?

But we still didn't know what shape our involvement would take. And it began to make us think about visiting Israel. But that was a pipe dream. The farthest from New York I had ever been was Florida, years earlier. We began to pray about it and kept the thought tucked away. Then one beautiful April afternoon, about a year after that conference, I was on my usual three-mile walk when a thought surprised me. "*Barbara, get your passport.*" But Israel was something we imagined way in the future. We had little money, not even the 180 dollars needed to get both of our passports. So I just ignored the notion.

Three months later, I was on my way to the grocery store. The traffic was stop and go, and a pickup truck rear-ended my station wagon. An officer came to the scene, and we filled out all the paper work. My tail light was damaged, but other than that, the car was okay. Roman found a part in a junk yard and fixed the tail light. In October, a check came from the insurance company for almost 1,000 dollars.

A few months after that, Mom Detweiler called to say that she was going to visit her daughter, Carol, in Sao Paulo, Brazil. Mom was seventy-seven at the time, and the flight would be long, about ten hours. I felt as though the Lord wanted me to go with her. The cost for my ticket was almost exactly what we had received from the insurance company. Had I heeded what I then realized was the Lord's prodding six months earlier, I wouldn't have had to go through the hassle and expense of getting my passport in just two weeks.

We left for Brazil a few days after Christmas. We stayed in Sao Paulo with Carol for nearly three weeks, shopping, enjoying the weather, and savoring that famous Brazilian coffee. Toward the end of our trip, we visited Rio de Janeiro, famous for its beaches and Corcovado Mountain, where a concrete statue of Christ, arms outstretched, embraces the city. This 100-foot tall figure is one of the most famous symbols of Rio and is visible night and day from most of the city's neighborhoods. As we wound our way up to what seemed like the clouds in a tour bus, I felt as though the Lord Himself had carefully orchestrated this trip—that the nagging to get my passport, the fender bender, and the insurance check had all been part of a larger plan. And I knew in my spirit that this was just a dress rehearsal and that I was being prepared for something. What I didn't know was that it would be of a magnitude that would dwarf the 2,300-foot mountain we were ascending.

Shortly after I got home, in mid-January of 1998, we received a pamphlet in the mail from Eagles' Wings, Robert Stearns' ministry. They were recruiting people for a trip to Israel in May. It was a logical next step in all that we had been feeling and involved with over the past five years. Roman and I felt and believed that the Lord was prompting us to go. But the cost would be nearly $5,000, and there was no way we could come up with that. So we prayed together, asking the Lord to provide if this was His will for us.

A sister at our church had known of our burden for Israel for years. When she heard of our desire to make this trip, she provided half the fare for us to go. We managed to borrow and scrape together the other half. For someone like me, who had only been to Florida once, two trips to two foreign countries in a matter of months was beyond my comprehension. On the verge of a journey we'd barely dared to dream about, I was filled with belief in the impossible. And my faith, much like that tour bus in Brazil, steadily climbed toward those outstretched arms.

On our first morning in the Holy Land, Roman and I woke before dawn to watch the sun rise over the Sea of Galilee. Standing on our hotel balcony, holding hands and praying, we asked the Lord to fulfill all that was in His heart in relation to the burden we felt. This burden had been repeatedly confirmed by what He was doing in our lives, especially by His enabling this trip. Never in our wildest dreams did we think we'd be gazing out at this holy water. It was the very sea where Peter and the disciples fished all night and caught nothing; where Jesus came and told them to cast their nets over the other side of their boat; and where, because they were following His instructions, their nets overflowed. At that moment, as we devoured the sunrise, only the Lord knew what was ahead for us. He knew that within a year, Roman and I would be the very fishermen that He would call to cast out His net for His people. And only the Lord knew how prophetic this trip would prove to be for us.

While in Israel, we visited the holocaust museum. The horror, sadness, and grief we experienced while there was later unbearably magnified when we spoke to, shared with, and helped repatriate many of the holocaust survivors from Ukraine.

We also watched a reenactment of the story of Ruth in the hills of Judea. Her words to Naomi, "Your people shall be my people, and your God my God" (Ruth 1:16), were the summation of all we felt in our hearts towards the Jewish people. They were the words that, as Christians, we would be paraphrasing to the Ukrainian Jews in less than a year.

One evening while we were in Jerusalem, a few of us from our tour group, along with Robert Stearns, walked to Liberty Park, which overlooks the citadel of David. Robert prayed that the Lord would open up the ancient wells of Abraham and release the prophetic voice of the Lord, and that we should ask God for the strategies of David, for the battles we fight are ancient ones. Roman and I didn't know it at that time, but we were about to face one of the most ancient battles of all—the fight to enable a second exodus of the Lord's people.

The most significant event of our visit to Israel happened at the Wailing Wall. As we arrived in the tour bus, tears spilled down our cheeks. It was as if this wall represented all the years that we'd carried our burden for the Jewish people and this nation. And now here we were, standing on the very ground where Jesus shed his blood, where history literally began.

Roman and I each had prayer requests from friends and family that were folded up on little pieces of paper. We separated, as is the custom for men and women for times of prayer, and placed the requests in cracks in the wall. When we found one another later, Roman still had tears in his eyes. When I asked him what he had prayed for, he said, "I asked the Lord to change my life." I froze, knowing that a change to his life meant a change to mine, and such an unspecific prayer in a place so holy frightened me. And not long after we returned home, God proved that "the effective, fervent prayer of a righteous man avails much" (James 5:16).

Everyone from church seemed interested in our trip, and we found ourselves repeating stories over and over. So we finally approached our pastor about sharing our experience as part of the service, which he was delighted to have us do.

We continued with our circle of friends who had a passion for Israel. We began to hold prayer meetings in our house, and sometimes guests from other churches would come and share and pray. As the months passed, Roman and I continued to reflect on our trip to Israel. Though we were Christians, experiencing the Holy Land had somehow made us feel Jewish, as if we had connected with some core part of ourselves that held us even more firmly to what we had been feeling for the past ten years. It was as if our internal "knower" uncovered the essence of who we were. And the desire for a mission trip was born.

At first we thought about going back to Israel. We felt like we wanted to go for longer, even for a few months. We itched to get underneath this thing that had hold of us, to experience the culture and nature of the people the Lord was calling us to. Being away for a few months would be doable. By this time, Shannon was married, Roman Eric was in college, and Keith was a junior in high school. But at the same time, the thought of leaving my children was unbearable. Throughout all these years, there had been two constants in our lives—our family and our calling. Not once did we think about choosing between them.

Through our network of friends, Roman and I discovered a ministry called Ebenezer Emergency Fund. They helped Russian Jews, primarily from Ukraine, with food and humanitarian aid. But their main focus was "Aliyah," helping the Jewish people return to Israel. Brochures and cassette tapes were passed along to us. We learned about Gustav Scheller, Ebenezer's founder, and how the Lord had laid this burden on his heart at a prayer conference in Israel during the Gulf War. We listened to powerful testimonies from volunteers who had worked with this organization. Even with all we'd learned and all the conferences we had attended, "Aliyah" was a new term for us. All I could think of was how I had felt in that holy land and how God's very own people must ache to get back there. And something primal took hold of me.

Over the next few months, we spoke of practically nothing but Ebenezer and how logical it seemed for the Lord to want to bring his people back to Israel. We began looking carefully into the Old Testament. We discovered prophecy after prophecy about how the Lord committed to bring His people home and how he'd send "fishermen" from the corners of the earth to "fish them" (Jeremiah 16:16). I'd go on my walks after work, and all I could think about was this ministry. *Is this what the Lord is calling us to?*

Roman and I began praying about this in the evenings after he came home from work. In January of 1998, we contacted the American coordinator of Ebenezer. He explained that this ministry was doing most of its work in Ukraine and that they had been there for seven years, bringing thousands of Jews home on ships that leave Odessa and go to Haifa, Israel. They were always looking for volunteers, and the commitment was no less than three months at a time. The volunteers' mission was to explain to the Jewish immigrants that Ebenezer was there to help them return to Israel and that through the Old Testament Scriptures the God of Israel was calling them back. And then the volunteers would help them actually make the trip.

Although Ebenezer is a Christian organization, they are adamant about not evangelizing the Jews. They explained that God was very clear when He gave His call to Gustav Scheller, the founder of the organization. It was simply, "Bring my people home."

After that conversation, Roman and I felt that this might be what we were being called to. So we submitted our applications, not knowing if or when we'd be accepted. Then about a month later, we began receiving mailings about a conference in Florida. It was called "The Israel Jubilee" and was to take place in April. Roman and I recognized that the Lord was directing us, but there was no money for such a trip. We'd need airfare, plus expenses for the four days of the conference. And Roman was reticent to ask for time off, as his boss depended heavily on him. But the more we prayed about it, the more we felt the Lord telling us that we should go.

Roman eventually did speak to his boss. And he not only gave Roman the green light to go, but also arranged for him to work the overtime that would pay, almost to the penny, for our airfare, meals, and attendance at the conference for four days. This was just the beginning of how God would provide, again and again, for what we needed, just when we needed it. One other example of this divine provision is that Shannon, to our delight, joined us. She had been closely following all that we had been involved in over the years and had developed a keen interest in our call to Israel. What she was exposed to during this conference helped to cement her blessing, as well as to influence her brothers' blessings, over our eventual decision to go overseas.

Part of the conference centered on Aliyah. Speakers shared about what our part was as the church and how this exodus would be far greater than the first. We actually met Gustav Scheller, and we told him that we had our applications in with his ministry to become volunteers in Ukraine. We heard him speak about how the Lord had begun this work in his heart in 1991 and how they had already brought thousands home by ship and plane. The Lord was putting form to all that had been in our hearts, and it was so much bigger than we ever imagined. Just the attendance at the conference alone spoke of the magnitude of this burden—there were over 12,000 people from around the world.

Gustav later played a video showing his organization at work, and our future suddenly became manifest right before our eyes. We were there, in the Ukrainian ghettos, delivering God's prophetic word to His people. We saw ourselves meeting the Jewish immigrants at the train stations; we carried their battered luggage aboard the ship at the Odessa port; we ministered to them during the time at sea, preparing them for their new lives in Israel.

Though we had spoken to the Ebenezer representative months earlier and had read about this work, the visual impact was consuming. It was as if the Lord had finally lassoed us in—as if all we'd experienced and had on our hearts over the past two decades had led up to this moment. And now we were being branded with His eternal desire.

Without a doubt, we knew what we were being called to do. And when I look back once again through those anointed binoculars, I see the twenty years it took for the Lord to bring us to this revelation as a time of discovery and enlightenment, of knitting our hearts to a single purpose. In retrospect, it was an easy time, especially compared to the next few months, when the Lord would need to carry us through all that this revelation would entail—leaving our home, our jobs, and our children.

Chapter 5 ❧

Preparing Head, Heart, and Home

Get out of your country, from your family and from your father's
house, to a land that I will show you.

—Genesis 12:1

ROMAN AND I were like children caught in the crest of a wave, our
everyday lives dwarfed by the confirmation of our call to Aliyah. But
our spiritual buoyancy subsided as we began to touch ground. We
were overwhelmed by how much of it had yet to be tilled. Up to this
point, all we had been involved with concerning Israel and the Jewish
people—the years of conferences, prayer meetings, and workshops—had
been integrated with and around our jobs, our home, and our family.
What we were now being called to do required a visceral yank from that
center of gravity.

When I speak about this time and people hear that Shannon had
just gotten married, Roman Eric was away at college, and Keith was
about to graduate, the reaction is, "Oh, that's good, at least your kids
were grown." As if the twanging of a parent's heartstrings has anything
to do with chronology. The thought of leaving my children pulled me
under every time.

Our frayed childhoods had estranged Roman and me from our
families. Because there were no grandparents, aunts, uncles, or cousins,
we intentionally knit close relationships with our children. The five of

27

us had become a universe unto ourselves, girded by the implicit promise to always be there for each other. If Roman and I went overseas, my greatest fear was that the fabric we had so carefully and lovingly woven would unravel. True, we were initially talking about being away for just three or four months, but it loomed like a hundred years.

Still, my marrow ached with the call to go and do this work. I felt that this opportunity might never be available again, that I needed to go while I could, while I had the energy and health. And yes, at a time the kids were old enough. Like David, I wanted to give the Lord something that cost me. But, oh God, I never dreamed I'd be faced with this—cut off from my children, half-way around the world with who knows what, if any, communication. It felt like my heart was being stretched and pulled like one of those Chinese finger traps. But if God told me to go, I wanted to be able to without hesitation. I wanted to have and walk in that kind of faith. Instead, I kept getting caught in an emotional riptide that, unbeknownst to me, was pulling Roman under too.

Roman was always the provider for our family. But committing to the work in Ukraine would mean he would have to quit his job. If it didn't work out overseas, he wouldn't be able to come back and collect unemployment. And if it did work out, what would he do once we returned? Keith was still in high school, graduating in a few months. He'd talked about going to community college, and we'd planned on using our savings, which wasn't much, to help pay for his education. But we'd need our savings for our airfare and expenses and to cover the mortgage and bills for the months we'd be gone. And both Keith and Roman Eric, who was in his second year of college on a scholarship, were on Roman's health insurance. Without his job, the boys would have no coverage. And neither would we.

For me to leave my job was nothing. I worked part time and just supplemented Roman's salary. But in a day when people are scrambling to gain the world, who, at fifty-three, walks away from everything? What kind of man sacrifices his son's education, risks his family's health, exhausts their finances, and jeopardizes a lifetime of security for three months as a missionary? I learned that it is the kind of man who, like Jacob, wrestles with God.

It was during our walks in the evenings, after he came home from work, that Roman began to share his heart, and it terrified me. In all the years I'd known him, this was the first time I'd heard him express fear. He'd never spoken much about his days in Vietnam. But during those walks he told me that what he was struggling with was more frightening than anything he'd faced on the battlefield, even more frightening than being shot. Back then, he would have been a single casualty. But this involved his family. None of his training as a marine had prepared Roman for the internal war that raged against his very manhood.

I tried to be supportive and encouraging, to help Roman through this time, until one night I heard a voice, very soft, right in my heart. *"Stop trying to convince him. Leave that to Me."* It is stunning when the Holy Spirit speaks. It doesn't happen very often, but when it does, it is a powerful reminder of the miracle living inside of us. After that, I became the best listener I could be.

Roman and I continued to pray together, many times with our faces to the floor. We asked the Lord for His grace and direction and to help us do this impossible thing of just letting everything go. The reality of what we faced was far beyond anything we imagined or were capable of dealing with by ourselves. We had no option but to trust the Lord. Only He could bring us through something of this emotional magnitude. And, sure enough, He did.

"Do you want to spend the rest of your life here?" Roman was at work when the words bore through his spirit. The tension and confusion that had mounted over the past weeks were replaced by certainty as Roman responded, "No, Lord, I don't." And then he remembered. At the Wailing Wall almost a year earlier, Roman had asked the Lord to change his life. And in his heart Roman knew that the wrestling, for now, was over.

Though Roman had received his green light from the Lord, I was still emotionally stuck every time I thought about leaving the kids. But just as twilight gives way to the rising sun, so God began to ease my anxiety. As if He were swaddling my spirit, I came to know that if we were obedient, if we went to find God's children and bring them home, that He would take care of ours. I came to know that He would provide for and protect our kids and minister to them when they worried about us and when they were lonely. I knew that the Lord was using our years as a family in Him to condition all of our hearts to accept what was before us.

What Roman and I were going to do had finally made its way from our heads to our hearts. Though it went against every natural instinct we had as parents and as logical, responsible adults, the emotional thrashing had quieted.

When our assigned dates came from Ebenezer, we knew right away that we had to change them. We had been slotted for May to September, but Keith was graduating in June. I called the day after our letter arrived, not knowing if we would still be considered if we had to change. But they said it wouldn't be a problem at all and rescheduled us for August through December. This gave us time to plan a small party for Keith and the rest of the summer to be with the kids and prepare for our trip. This was the first of many times the Lord would go before us, paving and smoothing the way.

We had been told by Ebenezer that we'd need multi-entry visas because the ship we would be working with would be making at least six trips from Odessa to Israel. So we sent our passports in to Washington, D.C. to apply for the visas. But when they came in the mail ten days later, we received double-entry visas, which meant we could exit and reenter Ukraine only once. We called Ebenezer, and they advised us to send the passports back and see if they'd reissue multi-entry visas for us. We did, but the passports came back the same way. We didn't know then that the Ukrainian government is very rigid and controlled with their visas and don't readily grant multi-entry visas. So we just thanked the Lord for what we did get, trusting that He was in control and that we got what we'd need.

After Keith's graduation party, we focused on what to bring overseas. We had been given a list, but the more we studied it, the more it seemed incomplete. We were told not to bring too much and were allowed only a certain weight on the plane. I thought of what it took to pack when we went to Virginia for just a week. How do you pack for four months in a country you know nothing about? As always, we prayed for wisdom and direction. We'd be in Ukraine during the winter, so we knew we'd need warm clothes and especially, good boots.

In all of this, we had to be frugal. Our budget was very limited, so shopping for what we needed was a challenge. I always prayed beforehand for the Lord to provide whatever it was I was looking for. One particular day, I asked Him to help me find a good pair of snow boots that I could afford and that wouldn't be too bulky to pack in a suitcase. Not expecting to find boots in the summer, I walked into a shoe store in one of our local outlets. To my right was a tall display with several shelves that were all bare, except for one, on which was a pair of snow boots. My heart in my throat, I walked over and checked the bottoms. They were my size and 50% off their $100 price tag. I sat down, tried them on, and cried. The boots fit perfectly, were fleece-lined, and made of soft, water-proofed leather that would be pliable for packing.

"Hi, Mrs. Fialkowski." I barely heard the voice above all the "Thank you, Lords" that filled my head. It was Kevin, Roman Eric's friend from high school. He'd spent many afternoons at our house after school playing basketball in the driveway. He worked at the store and gave me his 20% employee discount on top of the sale price. I walked out of that store with the perfect pair of boots for $29.00.

One thing after another fell into place like this. It was like having a Father looking out for your every need at the same time as He is stretching your faith to believe Him for provision. "And my God shall supply all your need according to His riches in glory by Christ Jesus" (Philippians 4:19). So much of the time we walk through life never knowing or experiencing the fullness of that ever-present, deep care and love. We get so wrapped up in our lives and ourselves that it takes something like this, some spectacular thing, to move us out of our complacency.

Besides packing, there was so much more to be done. We had to give away our plants, make sets of keys for Shannon and Keith, get a post office box for the mail, cancel magazine and newspaper subscriptions, and notify our neighbors. The list grew every day. I had to take each thing separately, deal with them one by one, no matter how small, before going on to the next. If I allowed myself to think about too much at once, I'd get caught in that riptide again.

Shannon agreed to handle our finances, so we had to arrange power of attorney and set up a small account for her. Keith would stay in the house while attending community college, so there was a list of household and other general instructions that also grew each day. These included reminders to turn down the thermostat at night; how to deal with any quirks in the appliances; and contact names and numbers for the plumber, electrician, and utility companies. Though there was some worry over leaving an eighteen-year-old boy on his own, Shannon and her husband, Billy, lived close by, and Keith and Billy were like brothers. Besides that, I had confidence that his being raised in the Lord had instilled in Keith the morals and values that would keep him out of trouble.

As the weeks went by, Roman and I used Shannon's bedroom to make piles of things we thought we'd need. I must have made fifty trips to that room every day, trying to eliminate something we didn't think was essential so that we'd meet the baggage weight requirement.

Although it wasn't on the packing list from Ebenezer, I sensed from the beginning that we should bring a small suitcase of food, that we'd need a measure of nutrition probably unavailable in Ukraine. I prayed about what to take and wound up with 15 cans of tuna fish, peanut butter, raisins, instant oatmeal, nuts, hot chocolate, instant soups, and six pounds of decaf coffee. When this suitcase was packed, it weighed about 31 pounds, which would limit our clothes. So we carefully eliminated, deciding on only those clothes we felt we'd need, especially for winter. In addition to all this, we took any antibiotics we had on hand, plus all the over-the-counter medicines we could think of. And someone had told us about the lack of toilet paper in Ukraine. So we folded our clothes around and in between twenty rolls of toilet paper. (I don't think I've ever been as glad about packing any item as I turned out to be about packing that!) Five days before we left, our suitcases were complete.

Now that the bulk of our preparation had been done, we had a few days to mentally and spiritually try to ease ourselves out of the only life we had ever known. During these few days, it occurred to Roman and me that we were alone in this. No one we knew had ever done anything like what we were about to do. Yes, we had met many who carried the same burden for Israel, but none who had actually walked away from their lives for the call of Aliyah. I thought about Abraham and about how this must have been what he felt like when God called him to leave his country and his family to go to an unknown land (Genesis 12:1).

Ebenezer had stressed the importance of having our church pray for us. They said that daily intercession was the backbone of their ministry and that intercessors from around the world prayed daily for the sailings. Before we left, we met with our pastors and explained this. And they did pray for us. But I sensed that they didn't fully understand what we were facing and how important their covering would be while we were away. And though everyone had been supportive, phone calls and visits became erratic in the weeks before we left. I began to feel a distance growing between our church and us.

Though the Christian church in general has a limited understanding about their relationship with Israel, our church had always grasped this. Our own enlightenment about God's heart for that nation had been birthed through this Fellowship. But in hindsight, the distance I was feeling had more to do with their limited understanding of Aliyah. And what I couldn't have known then was that when our work was finished more than two years later, this sense of isolation would return as a tsunami that would almost drown me.

On August 28, 1998, at 3:00 P.M., we pulled out of our driveway for the last time for four months. We wouldn't return until December 22, as we had decided to stay on in Jerusalem for an extra two weeks to work with the Christian Friends of Israel. From the back seat Shannon and Keith joked and shared anecdotes with the nonchalance of a trip to the grocery store. But like a dam about to burst, I could hear the trembling at the edge of their voices.

Once we were all checked in and through security, the four of us sat in the waiting area. It was pre-9/11, so the kids were allowed to come with us to the gate. It seemed like every few minutes I was telling

Shannon something about the house or the bills or the mail. Roman finally interrupted me, reminding me that it was all behind us now, and we needed to concentrate on what was ahead. He was right, of course, but I couldn't help myself. If I stopped talking, I would have to deal with the reality of the moment. Though as hard as it was, it would have been more difficult to stay behind when we knew the Lord had need of us overseas. And every time the thought of leaving the kids stabbed me, the Lord provided His amazing grace by countering with the reminder that He would take care of them.

The boarding call finally came. We all hugged and kissed like never before, each locking into the piece of the other that was about to be wrenched away. We looked into the faces of our children, our very likeness glistening beneath their tears. I don't think my heart had ever, or has ever since, withstood such a blow.

Roman spoke softly, compassionately, and with confidence. "We will see you in four months. Be good and take care of things." I could not speak a single word except, "I love you." They stayed with us in the boarding line right to the very end. Keith's arm was around Shannon. He was trying to be the big brother he knew she needed at that moment. We didn't want to hold up the other passengers, so we said our final, quick good-byes.

When the agent took our boarding passes, Shannon and Keith broke down. As we walked down the jet way, I could feel their eyes on our backs. I was about to turn around, wanting to see my children one last time. But before I could, the thought of Lot's wife leapt into my spirit: "But his wife looked back behind him, and she became a pillar of salt" (Genesis 19:26). So with Roman's hand on the small of my back, I forced myself to look straight ahead and obediently place one foot in front of the other.

Chapter 6

Strangers
in a Strange Land

How shall we sing the Lord's song in a foreign land?

—Psalm 137:4

"HE'S BANKING TO the left to make his approach for the landing."

Roman's voice roused me from an anxious half-sleep. Since leaving home, we had traveled nearly twenty hours, including the time change. Now, with the eight-hour flight to Austria and a four-hour layover behind us, we were finally arriving in Odessa. But exhausted as I was, any true rest had been kept at bay by the battle raging inside. Every time I closed my eyes, the faces of my children appeared like flares in a midnight sky. An army of unanswerable questions relentlessly attacked: *What if something happens to the kids? What if we run out of money? What if we get sick?*

I raised my head from Roman's shoulder and pulled his arm against my chest. Gazing out the window, he appeared totally absorbed in the mechanics of the Boeing 737's landing. But he sensed my fear and spoke softly over the top of my head. "God's in control."

As we came in for the approach, all I could see was cracked pavement flanked by what looked like sun-parched grass. When we landed and taxied down the runway, skeletons of helicopters and airplanes, stripped as clean as bones in a dessert, blurred passed us. It was as if we'd landed in an airport graveyard. When the plane stopped, I could see the terminal building in the distance. I had expected relief when we finally arrived in Ukraine, but the cold, gray facade of the Stalin era building only increased my anxiety. Even in bright sunlight it screamed, *Go home. You're not welcome here.*

As we unbuckled our seat belts and began to gather our belongings, I noticed that a stern-faced Ukrainian official had boarded the plane. When we made our way to the front, he checked our passports. I had never seen or heard of this type of security check before you even get off a plane. But it was the first of many such encounters in this country so recently under communist control.

The jalopy waiting to take us to the terminal was a testament to the poverty and oppression that characterized this country. Many seats were worn beyond belief, some missing, some with springs exposed. There was barely enough room for all of us, even when standing. I hung on to Roman with both hands, a small suitcase between my legs, and pulled my shirt up over my mouth and nose to avoid the diesel fumes.

At the terminal, we followed the swarm of bodies to a line that was forming inside. The cement-walled area contained no modern conveniences—no kiosks or computers, no conveyer belts for the luggage. The bags had been offloaded and stacked in a small, adjacent room. There were no chairs or benches, no signs or posters.

We heard only Russian. Though Roman could speak Polish, I knew it wouldn't be good enough in the weeks and months ahead. Roman again sensed my anxiety and spoke it down. "Don't worry. God's in control." I had to keep remembering that and reinforcing it with the promises of Scripture: "…casting all your care upon Him, for He cares for you" (1 Peter 5:7). It was a moment-by-moment struggle, but we had overcome the first major hurdle. We were here. And now I needed to, as the kids were fond of saying, stop talking the talk and start walking the walk.

The line was moving very slowly, and I needed a bathroom badly. I had learned enough Russian words and phrases before we left to be able to communicate my need. I left Roman with our place in line and followed the curt directions of one of the officers.

When I pushed the door to the bathroom open, I gagged. I stood in at least an inch of sewage water, and I chastised myself for not having gone on the plane. As my eyes became accustomed to the dimness, I saw that there were no seats on the toilets, no toilet paper, and no soap at the rusted sinks. Fighting the stench and the urge to leave, I knew I had little choice. I rummaged through my bag for some tissues, held my breath, and squatted over a bowl.

By the time I joined Roman in line, there was only one other person in front of him. In the weeks ahead I would lose all self-consciousness, but as we were called forward, I hoped no one noticed the damp rings at the bottom of my pants. Two stern-faced officials methodically scrutinized our visas and passports. Then they talked to each other in Russian. One of them surprisingly addressed us in English. He said that we needed to buy insurance, which would cost eighty American dollars. We hadn't been told anything about this. We barely had enough to make it through the four months, and this would be a significant blow. Fighting the burn of tears, I turned aside, again drawing upon the promise of Scripture. "Be anxious for nothing, but in everything by prayer and supplication, with thanksgiving, let your requests be made known to God" (Philippians 4:6).

Roman told the guards that this was our first time in the country, we were there as missionaries on a limited budget, and that we hadn't been told about the insurance. Smugly and arrogantly, they finally agreed for us to pay only eight dollars each and processed us into the country. Looking back, I see this was the first of many situations where God made a way where there appeared to be none—how He edified our faith just in time for us to overcome the next obstacle, which, as it happened, waited for us in the luggage area.

We handed an officer our claim tags, and within a few minutes, he brought three of our bags. But Roman's was missing, along with everything he needed for four months. Awake nearly a full day at this point, my stomach pitched watching Roman's swarthy complexion ashen. We had no idea what the procedure for lost luggage was, and even if we did, we wouldn't be able to communicate. Weariness slouching our shoulders, we were impatiently motioned toward the terminal area.

Typical Ukrainian toilet

The cold, gray, stadium-sized room seemed to immortalize the dark days of communism. I wondered how many westerners had passed through this room during those days and how the KGB must have scrutinized every traveler, much as we had been examined just moments ago. Lines snaked ticket counters, most people feeding the cloud of cigarette smoke that made it difficult for Roman and me to breathe. Many were old, the women's heads covered with scarves tied beneath their chins. I would later learn that these scarves are called "babushkas," a name commonly applied to any older, Russian woman. Like the room we had just left, there were no chairs or benches. Younger people leaned against each other or the walls. But the older people stood with a measure of discipline, like seasoned warhorses.

An Ebenezer volunteer was supposed to meet us, but it wasn't until that moment that we realized we had no idea what that person would look like. We had just been told that the person would find us. And sure enough, she did.

"Are you Roman and Barbara?" Startled, I turned to a pleasant-faced woman about my age. Relief fell like desert rain as she introduced herself as Shirley and her male, Russian translator as Patrice. The first thing we told her was about Roman's bag, that it contained all of his belongings, right down to the toothpaste. She assured us that this happens often and that other volunteers who had come through Austria had also lost bags. She said it sometimes takes a few days, but they are all eventually recovered.

Patrice spoke Russian, so he went to the appropriate desk and filed a missing bag report for us. Surprisingly, it only took a few minutes. Then we followed Shirley and him through the terminal to the Lorry (a van-like vehicle common in Ukraine), where we slumped together in the back seat for the ride to the base.

Ebenezer conducted its operations out of an old Communist youth camp. It was a dormitory setup, with five bedrooms on the ground floor and four on the second. Our room was cramped, with two single beds, a dresser, and a small wardrobe. A cloudy window draped with flimsy curtains was above the beds. We had our own, small bathroom. It had a tiny tub, about 40 inches square with eight-inch sidewalls and an open shower.

We had arrived just before supper, after which was the nightly eight o'clock meeting. I was too tired to eat much, and I don't even remember what was served. We attended the meeting, but by that time, I was past the point of retaining anything. Everything was spoken in two languages, first Russian and then English. I asked Roman to pay attention, as it was all I could do just to stay upright. The meeting ended around 10. I had never been so grateful for a bed.

We had spent our first night in Ukraine. I opened my eyes to sun streaming through the aged window, barking dogs, and conversations in Russian. I felt rested and much more alert than the day before. We had about an hour before breakfast, which was to be served at nine. Using threadbare towels, we washed up in cold water. I made a mental note to ask about that at breakfast.

I had been too tired the night before to fully take in our surroundings. The dining room seemed as if it could hold about 70 people. There were huge murals on the rear wall depicting life in Odessa—an opera house, the train station, the Black Sea. There was also a small stage with a piano, which I thought was unusual. But later I was told that Ebenezer just rented the space and that weddings and community events also took place there.

We met up with Shirley, whose job partly was to stay with the newcomers and help get them adjusted. Within minutes of sitting down at a table, a "babushka" brought our breakfast. We were given bowls of cooked rice in milk, bread and butter, potatoes (either fried or mashed), and eggs. Though not what we were used to, the meal was hot and fresh. The bread was especially good.

Over breakfast, Shirley gave us the low down as to life on the base. There was hot water only three times a week: Monday, Wednesday, and Friday between 8 and 10 P.M. The hot water lasted only about two hours for 30 volunteers, so showers had to be quick. There was no hot water at all during the day. I was so glad I had brought a small, electric tea kettle with us so that we could at least have tea.

During breakfast, Roman and I met the volunteers who, like us, had come to work from August through December. There were thirty total, fifteen Ukrainian and fifteen from different western countries. Five of us were from America—Roman and me, one other couple from South Carolina, and a young man from Texas. It felt so good to be able to speak English with them. Some volunteers from the other countries spoke English too, but many Ukrainians didn't. Over the course of our time there, we wound up using our own made-up sign language for almost everything, which was very comical.

That first day was spent getting familiar with our surroundings. After breakfast, about six of us set out on foot to the local market. It was like walking through a history book, back to the beginning of the cold war. We left the base through a heavy, iron door, which was connected to a gate enclosure about eight feet high that surrounded the grounds. Similarly, the small, dilapidated houses spotting either side of the unpaved road were barricaded by eight to ten feet of cement or wood fencing. Ironically, these walls of protection had stood the test of time, while everything within and without had deteriorated. Grass was weedy and unkempt, as if it had never been mowed. Broken glass and garbage were strewn about the road. Tree branches stuck up from potholes to alert drivers. Dogs were everywhere, ribs prominent, sniffing through trash. People walked with their heads down, as if not wanting to engage their surroundings or anyone in them.

Near the market were some apartment buildings. As we got closer, they appeared to be nothing but cement slabs stacked on top of each other. Roman said there probably were no steel support beams in the construction. People we assumed were tenants, many elderly, rested on broken, wooden benches in front of the apartments. It surprised me how much of this population seemed to be at least twenty years older than Roman and me and how the government appeared not to care at all about the conditions they lived in. We ached as we observed the poverty and hopelessness around us. And this was just our first day, our first hours there. In the weeks and months ahead, we would feed on God's grace to enable us to survive the magnitude of the need and the mounting compassion that would continue to threaten our work.

The Odessa Marketplace

The market area was the size of a football field, with back-to-back vendors selling goods on tarps on the ground. We entered through the fish section, the stench like rotting garbage. I followed Shirley's lead, pulling my shirt collar up over my nose. Flies were everywhere, especially on the food. There were crates of meat out in the August sun and wild dogs sniffing around. I couldn't believe there were no health codes about fish, meat, and perishable food being sold without refrigeration.

There were booths selling bottled water, soda, and milk, which we needed. The water wasn't fit to drink in Odessa, and we hadn't yet hooked up the small water purifier we had brought from the States. The milk was sold in small, cardboard containers that didn't need refrigeration. Shirley assured us that it was drinkable and safe. As we paid for what we needed, I was thankful I'd brought those few food items.

Shirley had been there for four years, so over the next two days, I took my cues from her, watching her closely. We made a few more trips to the market and met the full team and everyone we'd be working with over the next four months. There was only one computer for the volunteers, but everyone was patient and understanding when it came to receiving emails or getting them out. Initially, the hot water situation was hard to get used to. We took so much for granted back home. But as we began to get caught up in the work, showering became secondary.

Our first assignment began on the third day. Our tasks were explained through a translator the night before in the meeting after dinner. We were part of a team that was to help four families (referred to as "Olim," or Jewish immigrants) who were making Aliyah transport their belongings to the port of Odessa. We had to go to each family's apartment and bring their baggage to the port, where it would be searched and weighed by the authorities. Then we were to put it all into big, wooden crates and write names, passport numbers, and destination (Haifa) on each crate. Everything would then be ready for loading on the day of their sailing. It all sounded organized and doable.

We rose at 5:30, had prayer at 6:15, and ate breakfast at 6:30. By 7:00, we were on our way in the Lorry. We had general addresses for the apartment complexes, but what we didn't know was that the complexes were like small towns. There were no specific directions for locating our families, no building or apartment numbers. Once we reached

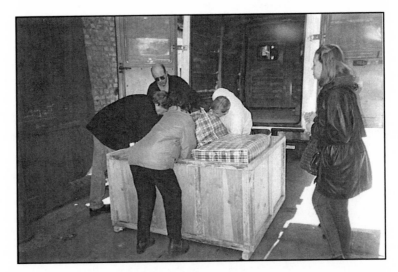

Packing crates at Odessa Port

a complex, we stopped and asked people, through our Russian team leader, if they knew how we could find such-and-such a family. They stared blankly and shook their heads slightly, as if they didn't know or care who or what we were talking about. At one point, after more than an hour of driving around one of the complexes, we just stopped the Lorry and prayed, believing that the Lord would help us. Shortly afterwards, a babushka approached the Lorry and helped us find our first family. They, in turn, gave us some help in finding the others. This was the way we would learn to live over the next four months—completely dependent on the Lord.

Every building was run down, seemingly on the verge of collapse. Some families lived on the upper floors in buildings that didn't have elevators. And in the buildings that did, we had to use the stairs because of an electrical outage that morning. These were frequent in Odessa and lasted for hours at a time. Without lights, you could barely make out your steps. Some of the stairs were broken or had risers missing. I was afraid of tripping or falling, imagining myself with broken limbs in a backward Ukrainian hospital. I found myself questioning what we were doing, what we had committed to. But I knew that if I allowed this mindset to continue, I would become a casualty in this work.

It was on this first day of work that I began to flex my spiritual muscles in ways I never had before. As I made my way up the stairs, Scripture verses made their way up from my heart. I took "every thought into captivity to the obedience of Christ" (2 Corinthians 10:5) and remembered why we were here: "If any of you are driven out to the farthest parts under heaven, from here the Lord your God will gather you, and from there He will bring you" (Deuteronomy 30:4). And then the grace came.

When we reached our first family's apartment, we were met by nodding heads, expectant eyes, and eager smiles. It wasn't uncommon for a family to have eight or more bags, some weighing as much as eighty pounds. Two of us on the team were women, so we took the smaller bags. They seemed like a hundred pounds to me but were probably more like thirty or forty. We had to grab the handles with both hands and take each step of the five or six flights singly, placing both feet on each step before proceeding to the next. In the darkness of the stairway, again fearful of missing a step and falling, I thanked God for rooting His Word so deeply within me. I was reminded that "I can do all things through Christ who strengthens me" (Philippians 4:13).

Most of the heavier luggage had straps. The men used these to put their arms through and carry the bags on their backs, like backpacks, so that the weight would be behind them as they went down the stairs. Roman was the new man on the team and sometimes got left with the heaviest bags. It hurt to watch him carry a bag down the five flights of stairs, load it on the Lorry, then go back up to get another. I had no idea the work would be this physical, this back breaking (literally). I thanked God that I had built up an aerobic endurance with all my years of walking and that Roman's time as a marine had motivated him to keep up his exercise and weight training. At this point, we had no idea that what was up ahead for us would require so much more than just physical endurance.

Within a few hours, we had loaded the belongings of all four families. One family's total belongings, everything they had in the world, amounted to one tattered suitcase and a cardboard box. We took one member of each family to the port with us so that they could answer any questions about their paperwork. It was here that I began to see the enormity of what it took to get these Jewish people out of the country.

Proper paperwork in Ukraine is like gold. In hindsight, I see it is a miracle that Ebenezer is able to help secure birth certificates and working papers so that the Olim can get their passports. So many of these families either had documents destroyed during World War II, or they themselves destroyed them, changing their names in an attempt to avoid persecution. The fact that the staff of Ebenezer was able to get this documentation together made me feel as if God Himself was directing the work. "Heap it up! Heap it up! Prepare the way, take the stumbling block out of the way of My people" (Isaiah 57:14).

At the port, you had to show identification at all entry and exit points. The family members we brought with us were elderly, and they had to endure lengthy scrutiny of their documents. Officials went through their paperwork line by line, reinforcing that spirit of control we would confront time and again. They had to make you aware that they were in charge. But the Olim making Aliyah didn't flinch at the waiting. It was as if they had done it all their lives. We were learning that waiting was the fabric of life in this nation.

When we were finished at the port, we took the family members back to their flats and then returned to the base around 1:00 P.M., in time for lunch. The morning's work had made us ravenous. Lunch was always soup, no matter how hot the weather. It was mostly broth, but good, with just a few vegetables or small pieces of meat. And there'd be some fried fish or potatoes and bread. The portions were small, and I worried that it wouldn't be enough, especially for men like Roman, who were used to hearty eating. And I knew that the work ahead of us would require more energy than this food would provide. After lunch I usually brought some bread back to our room so we could have a peanut butter sandwich later on. I was so grateful for that source of protein and so glad I'd brought it along. At dinner, I always brought my peanut butter with me, and I'd share it with the volunteers. Sometimes the food, whether chicken, meat, or fish, would be swimming in so much fat that I just couldn't eat it. Roman, on the other hand, ate everything and seemed to enjoy it.

In spite of the food, I looked forward to mealtimes. It was then that the work was behind us, and no matter how hard or emotionally wrenching it had been, the camaraderie of this ragtag group made it all fall away. The mix of languages and made-up sign language translated into something we could all understand—laughter. Being brought together like that for a work so much bigger than all of us was so like the Lord...and like nothing we have ever known since.

After lunch, we usually headed to the office to try and get a few quick emails out. They were like manna from heaven, as the computer was the only link we had with the outside world. The Ukrainians would let us know if something was going on internationally that seemed important, but half the time they didn't seem to care. The long years of communism seemed to have molded them to total surrender to whatever was happening, as if they accepted what was going on because there was nothing they could do about it. It seemed to be a fear-based submission that I especially noticed among the Olim. They'd cower in certain situations and back off when any kind of authority exerted itself. It was as if this nation was shrouded in a canopy of oppression and depression.

Our next assignment was to go to the Odessa train station and pick up the Olim who were making Aliyah from different parts of Russia and Ukraine. Then we were to bring them, with their luggage, to their assigned Ebenezer base for an orientation before their sailing date, which was usually a week later. Roman and I were assigned to a team of six that was led by a Russian, who drove the Lorry.

As we boarded the Lorry at 5:30 A.M., our cheery "good mornings" were met by stony silence. The demeanor of the Russian volunteers, especially of the team leaders, was hard for me to get used to. I realize now that it was just our cultural differences. I had to keep reminding myself that we were in what used to be Soviet Russia, a spiritual vacuum, where years of emotional bondage still had a hold, and that despite our personality differences, we were all Christian volunteers knit by a single purpose—to bring the Jewish people home to Israel.

As we drove to the train station, I was surprised by how many people were already on the streets waiting for trolleys and buses. It was September now, still mild, the sun just coming up. I thought of autumn at home. About how, after the laze and haze of summer, the air cleared, the months held promise, and the light popped colors into focus, as if you had slipped on a pair of 3-D glasses. But here in Ukraine, the air was dusty and desperate, and the light fell on a colorless landscape, a gray-brown mural of dilapidated buildings, broken benches, and pot-holed roads.

Old babushkas were out on the streets and sidewalks with small brooms. They ceaselessly swept back and forth, making sure to get every piece of debris, every leaf. Their lined faces held a sad resignation, as if their hopes and dreams had been relegated to the dirt, swept and tucked into the crevices of broken cement and road. I thought of the huge street-sweeping trucks back home, and I had the urge to stop the Lorry, get out, and give these women some money for their work. But

I knew that money would not change what needed to be done in the hearts and spirits of these people.

My own heart began to fill with a compassion that frightened me. I realized that without grace, without an anointing in the midst of this brokenness and despair, we wouldn't be able to accomplish what we came to do.

We arrived at the station a few minutes after six. There were luggage trolleys in the back of the van, and we wheeled them onto the platform to wait for the first train. The Odessa train station dated back to the war and accommodated people throughout Ukraine, Russia, and Poland. The terminal was a stucco building, two stories high, with huge, arched windows. Enormous wrought-iron gates guarded the entrance to the platforms.

As we waited, music piped through loudspeakers. Its tinny timbre sounded like something out of an old World War II movie. My flesh crawled as I realized that these were the same platforms where, just fifty years earlier, German soldiers had probably stood waiting to take trainloads of Jews to their slaughter. And here we were, Christians of all ethnicities, including German, waiting to take trainloads of Jews to Israel, to safety, to a better life. How honored and humbled we were to be fulfilling God's promise as prophesied in Isaiah 11:12: "He will set up a banner for the nations, and will assemble the outcasts of Israel, and gather together the dispersed of Judah from the four corners of the earth."

In the week before the first sailing, we made several trips to the train station, picking up twelve to fifteen people each trip. It was like being in a time machine, observing a slice of humanity forgotten and forsaken by everyone but God.

The families were bedraggled; some of them had been traveling for days. They were young and old and everything in between. The older women all seemed to be short and stocky, the familiar babushka tied beneath their chins. Some wore simple coats of gray, brown, or black over

Odessa train station

Roman picking up Olim at the station

dresses that fell well past their coat hems. Several were in wheelchairs, some on crutches. Their calves were thick and straight, ending in swollen ankles that billowed over worn, laced shoes. They appeared to give way to the men who, although clothed just as shabbily, held a measure of purpose and determination that was absent in the women. No one, except the children, smiled. I supposed their sense of adventure had escaped the years of smothering bondage endured by their elders.

Each family had their earthly belongings packed into crates, boxes, and battered suitcases. Many arrived with cats and dogs, some on leashes, some in crates. There was even a cat named Moses making Aliyah to Israel! All this made me think of Noah's ark—not so much because of the animals, but because of the sense of escape that exited those trains, as if each car breathed a sigh of relief when it opened its doors and spilled the Olim onto the platform.

Like the families in the apartments, each of these families averaged eight heavy pieces of luggage. The trolleys were small and sometimes could only take one bag or crate at a time. Even with six of us, this was exhausting. But the people were precious and clearly trusted us, literally, with their lives. We continually asked the Lord to give us not only the physical strength to carry their luggage, but also the spiritual strength to help carry and bear their burdens. For the first of many times, we began to see the fulfillment of Isaiah 49:22: "Behold, I will lift My hand in an oath to the nations, and set up My standard for the peoples; they shall bring your sons in their arms, and your daughters shall be carried on their shoulders."

Once the Olim and their luggage were loaded onto the Lorry, we drove them to their assigned base. There we waited while they checked in at the office. They had to show their passports and paperwork and all the necessary information about family members traveling with them. Once they were assigned a room, we'd deliver their luggage.

The rooms were plain but spacious and could accommodate a family of five. If there were more than five, a family would be given two rooms. The décor was drab with just the essentials—beds, a dresser, and maybe a chair or two. But as they entered these temporary havens, the Olim's wide-eyed wonder told us it was more than what most of them had come from. Some had traveled for days from remote parts of Russia and would use the week ahead to rest and prepare for their journey to Haifa.

As the time for the first sailing from our base drew near, we were filling up with Olim. As the numbers increased, volunteers were assigned to help with any special care the people needed. Some helped with children, others with the older people who required assistance walking or with their wheelchairs.

During this time, Roman and I got to know some of the people very well. Through our broken Russian, Roman's Polish, and the base translators, we were able to help settle some of their fears about leaving the country and their relatives behind. Reaching into Scripture, we knelt in front of them; held bony, trembling hands; and tried to reassure them that once they got settled in Israel, it would be easier for Ebenezer to get their relatives over, should they want to come. "Strengthen the weak hands, and make firm the feeble knees. Say to those who are fearful-hearted, 'Be strong, do not fear! Behold, your God will...come and save you'" (Isaiah 35:3–4).

Many of the elderly had never known anything but Russia, communism, and in many cases, persecution. The fact that these people, some well into their eighties, were here and on their way to their promised land spoke absolutely of God's promise through Isaiah: "Even to your old age, I am He, and even to gray hairs I will carry you!...and will deliver you" (Isaiah 46:4). Having just left our own country and family weeks earlier, Roman and I thought how much like the Lord this was—to already be using our time of trial for His glory. He had given us the grace to minister to these people with compassion that was heartfelt and healing.

Over the course of the week, Roman and I were surprised by how many of the Russian children knew English words. They did not know enough to communicate fluently, but enough to help us understand what they were trying to get across. We'd find ourselves looking forward to seeing these kids each day, to hearing the precious, heavily accented words and phrases that pricked our hearts. We'd give them hugs, pick them up, and play make-shift games of basketball with anything that resembled a hoop. And then they'd start looking for us, eager for another piece of chocolate or gum, which we kept in our pockets just for them. By the time the sailing came around, we had become like their grandparents.

In the days before the sailing, Roman and I would often take walks to the Black Sea, a short distance from the base. Many of the Olim and their children did the same. We watched them sit by the water, and we knew they were preparing their hearts for the journey ahead. You could see the excitement in their body language and in their hand gestures as they talked. Many had never been out of the country, and surely they had never had an experience like this.

At any one time before the sailing, there could be upwards of 100 people on the base. With hot water only three days a week for a two-hour span, showering became an Olympic event. But through it all, the air crackled with excitement, voices were at a fever pitch, and energy levels were palpable.

.

Chapter 7 ↷

Preparing
for the First Sailing

Unless the Lord builds the house, they labor in vain who build it.
—Psalm 127:1

WE'D BEEN IN Odessa for two weeks. During that time, between
Roman's Polish and the few Russian words and phrases we had mastered,
we had been able to communicate. But as sailing day approached, the
Russian volunteers who were in charge might as well have been speaking
in tongues. A few times, their frenzied exchanges moved us to pull a
translator aside to find out what was going on. When we did, our eyes
reopened to the enormity of what we were up against.

Think about what it takes to get yourself or your family off on a
vacation for a week or two. Aside from packing, there's the planning,
the preparation, and the tying up of loose ends associated with leaving
your home—consideration of pets, newspapers, mail, utilities, social
commitments, etc. Now think about packing up, transporting, and
entirely relocating 400 lives. I guess we never had really thought too
much about what was involved with this move. We just knew that we'd
be helping God's people get to Israel via ship. When the translator
conveyed the logistics and details, our jaws dropped in a holy awe that
verged on disbelief. Even without our realizing that this number would

multiply forty times before our work was done there, the effort before us seemed nothing short of a modern-day Exodus.

None of the volunteers had any experience with something of this magnitude. We were a ragtag group of people who spoke different languages and hailed from different cultures. Our only, but binding, connection was what God had placed on our hearts—to bring His people home. It was the same call God had given Gustav Scheller in the 1991 prayer conference that birthed Ebenezer's ministry, the same call God had given Moses over 3,000 years ago. And, like Moses, we were in dire need of the miraculous. As we began to understand this seemingly impossible move, we knew that the Olim were our Israelites, the Ukrainian government was the Egyptians, and to get these people home, God would have to all but part the Black Sea.

The volunteers who were organizing the sailing had responsibilities I was grateful weren't ours. They had to make sure that every document, every ship manifest held up under the scrutiny of the port officials. These officials were people who took pleasure in finding fault. In fact, they made a special effort to do just that. If any little thing was out of order on sailing day, it could mean hours of delay and anxiety for everyone.

We found out that separate manifests had to be completed for the Olim, for the volunteers who were sailing, for the animals, and for the crates and luggage. Each item of baggage had to be weighed, as there were limits on how much each person or family was allowed to take on board. Wheelchairs, walkers, and crutches also had to be recorded on separate manifests. If an Olim or a family had anything that wasn't accounted for or if their paperwork wasn't in order, it could result in their not being able to make the trip and having to wait until the next sailing.

About a week prior to departure, each Olim had to be interviewed to make sure that all of their traveling documents were up to date and in order. If not, someone would be assigned to scurry around to the appropriate agencies, in many cases having to bribe officials with money, chocolate, or soda, in order to expedite whatever was needed.

In addition to the paperwork, the volunteers had to be concerned about those Olim who were elderly, sick, or disabled (some blind). They would need special attention on board, and volunteers would have to be assigned to them. There was always a concern as to whether or not these Olim would be physically able to make the trip. Also, judgments had to be made so we knew if medical help would be needed at the port in Haifa, and if so, arrangements had to be made ahead of time.

As the translators relayed all of this to us, we understood the heightened concern, frenzy, and anxiety that continued to mount as departure day approached. With all that was being revealed about the process, with the craziness and chaos that preceded the sailing, it was hard to keep assured spiritually. I began to get scared and really question the whole process. I couldn't imagine getting everyone, with their luggage and pets, just from the base to the port, let alone through customs and on and off the ship. So I had to remember that our being there and doing what we'd already done in these short weeks was truly a testament to God's grace over our lives. Because without His grace, we wouldn't have been able to leave our children and our home, risk all that was safe and familiar, and travel to this time-warped nation to walk out four-thousand-year-old prophecies. In order to keep going forward, we had to remember that "with God all things are possible" (Matthew 19:26). We had to live by faith, plain and simple.

The night before the sailing, there were two meetings. The first was a "farewell meeting" for the Olim. The second meeting was for the volunteers—for those who would be going on the sailing and for those, like Roman and me, who would be going to the port only to help load people and luggage. Our visas limited us to only one sailing during our stay. That sailing was scheduled in another two weeks, after our first "fishing trip," which Roman and I were going on two days after this ship left.

The farewell meeting was held in the main dining room after dinner. The tables were folded and put to the side, and rows of chairs were set up. One of the Russian volunteers kicked off the meeting by giving information about sailing day. He explained the procedures for getting to the port, including the time the buses were to arrive and in what order the Olim were to board. He also explained our responsibilities to the

Olim—some of us would help with luggage, some with getting their documents reviewed, and others would be sailing with them.

Scores of attentive faces, each with a unique expression, were locked on the speaker. Some appeared incredulous, as if they could not imagine what this move would mean for them. Some looked resigned, as if they didn't really care; they just wanted to get out of this oppressive, anti-Semitic place. Others seemed eager for freedom, something they had never really known. I believe many wanted a chance to begin afresh, while others wanted only to die in Israel. Ages ranged from infants to pregnant women to those well into their eighties. Some of the elderly were without sight and a few were unable to walk unassisted. Had I not seen it myself, I would have thought it impossible for people that age and in those conditions to change countries and cultures. Yet here they were, before my eyes, miraculously proving the Lord's promise: "Behold, I will bring them from the north country, and gather them from the ends of the earth, among them the blind and the lame, the woman with child and the one who labors with child..." (Jeremiah 31:8).

After the Olim were given their instructions for the following day, two of the western volunteers who were going on the sailing were asked to share a testimony of what brought them to Ukraine. As they began to explain their love for the Jewish people and how God had put it on their hearts to come and help, the sea of faces that moments ago bore witness to individual experiences and circumstances now blended into one expression of intimacy, awe, and wonder. It was as if, were it not for the reality that the speakers were living, the Olim wouldn't have believed that these volunteers had actually been called by God to help them.

As I listened to how the Lord had worked in the lives of these other volunteers, I realized how we were all really just nobodies in the natural world. But through the same desire burning inside all of us, we had become His eyes, hands, feet, and heart. I realized, not for the first time, that God "is the same yesterday, today and forever" (Hebrews 13:8), and that we can stand on His promises—all of His wonderful promises. I pondered how, in utter awe and humility, we stood in the epicenter of this promise, so much greater and bigger than any of us. As it says in Jeremiah 3:18, "...and they shall come together out of the land of the north to the land that I have given as an inheritance to your fathers."

Once the volunteers had shared, we celebrated with singing and dancing. Some songs were sung in Hebrew, and some of the volunteers, like me, played guitar or other instruments. We finished up with "Hava Nagila," which was played on a tape cassette so that the volunteers could join in the dancing with the Olim.

Gap-toothed, gold-crowned smiles brightened the room as the Olim felt special and honored to be dancing with us. Some were crying, realizing the love we had for them and this work. They weren't used to seeing and feeling love expressed through simple people like us. In fact, I'd venture to say that they weren't used to seeing and feeling love expressed at all. In that country and culture, people seemed to have very little respect for one another, especially for the Jews.

Though Ebenezer is a Christian ministry, we weren't allowed to proselytize our faith in any way other than through the prophetic words of Scripture that we were living out. But it was so obvious through the joy in that dining hall that whether they had believed in God before or not, whether they had ever heard the name of Jesus before or not, these Olim were declaring "…the praises of Him who called you out of darkness into His marvelous light" (1 Peter 2:9).

The next meeting was for the volunteers. Those who were going on the ship to Haifa were obviously excited. And after having spoken with some who had already sailed, we understood why. On board the ship, hot water was always available. You could bathe and take a shower any time you wanted to. The food was good, fresh, well-prepared, and abundant. I found myself wishing we were going with them, fantasizing about fresh, hot coffee, no power losses, and endless showers.

I snapped back to reality as names began to be called. First, each volunteer who was going on the sailing was given a boarding card with his or her name and cabin number. As they went up to get their cards, their excitement about connecting with the real world again left us a bit envious. We had no access to TV, radio, or newspapers, so we were sure to

Farewell meeting for the Olim on base

ask the volunteers to bring back an English newspaper from Haifa—even though by the time we'd get it, the news would be a week old

We were all given written instructions with a picture of a ship and lists of five work teams. The first team was made up of the leaders responsible for the buses to the port from the base. The second was those who were traveling on the ship and would be responsible for overseeing that the luggage got to the proper cabins. The third team was assigned to the wharf, where luggage would be taken from the trolleys and up the gangplank to the ship. The fourth team was assigned to the waiting hall, where all the Olim would queue up to pass through customs and where bags would be put through x-ray machines. The fifth team was assigned to the customs hall, where the Olim would be processed and luggage would be pushed through on trolleys for loading onto the ship. Each team had at least eight people, more for those on the wharf. Roman was on the wharf with the third team, and I was on the fifth team with the trolleys. On paper, it all seemed organized and doable. The reality was another thing.

We woke at 5:30 and had breakfast with the Olim at 6:00. The "kitchen ladies," as we called them, brought the food around to the table on trays. There were eight of them, and they prepared three meals a day for over a hundred people. Compared to most of the Russians, they were very gracious. And it amazed me how early they had to rise to prepare this food.

One morning, about a week earlier, I had asked to see the kitchen. And then I was sorry I did. The good thing was the teamwork I witnessed. Though they all served, there were obvious responsibilities in the kitchen. Some were preparing, some cooking, some washing dishes. But the scene, again, was something from the cold war. The stoves and ovens seemed at least fifty years old. And everything was done by hand. There were no appliances—food processors, mixers, or dishwashers. Also, everything was washed not only by hand, but also with cold water and just a small amount of soap.

I tried not to think about my trip to the kitchen as I scanned the choices on the trays. There was usually some fish or sardines with a pickle or tomato slice, a piece of cheese, some watery semolina cereal, eggs, or yogurt. It was too early for fish, too early for me to eat, actually. But I

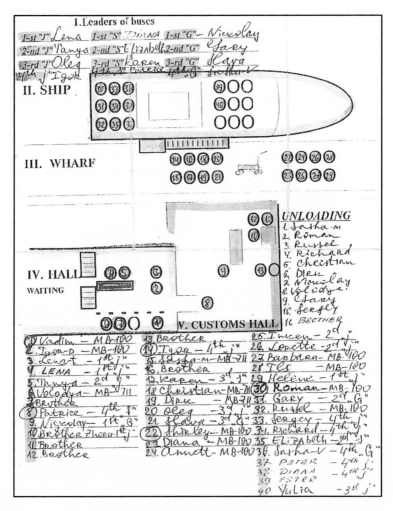

Volunteers' work on the day of sailing

knew I needed something for the work ahead, so I chose some yogurt and bread with jam.

Conversations and excitement were at a high, the children noisier and wilder than usual. By 6:30, just as the sun poked over the horizon, the clattering of dishes and silver signaled the end of breakfast. We could hear the buses' snorting engines and the screeching and scraping of the big green trolleys as the Olim and volunteers began transporting their luggage from their rooms.

By the time Roman and I finished breakfast, there were already lines of Olim and luggage waiting to board. Roman and the other men helped load the bags into the compartment on the bottom of the bus. Each bag was a minimum of eighty pounds, so just loading one bus was exhausting. On practically every bus, bags had to be loaded onto the back of the bus itself as the luggage compartments filled.

There would be nine buses that morning, arriving three at a time. Roman and I were assigned to the first group. As volunteers, we let the Olim have the seats, and we stood on the ride to the port. I don't do well in crowds, especially in cramped spaces like the bus we were on. But the Lord's grace eased my discomfort with the joyful, high-pitched Russian that swirled around me. The children's faces were filled with questions, and when they looked at me, I'd just smile and pat their little heads, hoping to give them some reassurance. They were going home! And no one but the Lord would get the glory for this work. "'There is hope in your future,' says the Lord, 'That your children shall come back to their own border'" (Jeremiah 31:17).

We arrived at the port and, along with the other volunteers, began unloading the heavy bags, one by one, onto the sidewalk next to the bus. We came with a group of three busloads, and there were six more expected. Each bus averaged about fifty Olim and a minimum of 100 bags.

The Olim were directed to go inside the port building to a large, open area, find a place to sit, and then retrieve their luggage once it was brought inside. There was a stairway of about fifty steps at the entrance to the port building. In order to get the hundreds of pieces of luggage up the steps, down a corridor of about 300 feet, and into the area where the Olim waited, the volunteers made a human chain. Each bag was passed from one person to the next. We started at the bus and then went up the steps and down the corridor. When we got the bags inside, we slid them along the hallway to the waiting area, being careful with their belongings.

I watched the men, including Roman, veins popping on arms and necks, knuckles white, hefting bags up the steps. This archaic process was unbelievable, especially when I saw an escalator, practically brand new, right alongside the stairway. The authorities wouldn't allow us to use it, as they said the weight of the luggage would break it. This was the "Egyptian" mentality we were up against—stubborn, prideful, and brutal. Every time you turned around, it seemed this culture was in your face, increasing the difficulty of whatever situation you were in. But we were in the Lord's army in this effort. "Be strong and of good courage, for to this people you shall divide as an inheritance the land which I swore to their fathers to give them" (Joshua 1:6). So we cheerfully passed the bags along, had some crazy conversations in broken bits of each other's languages, and without even understanding each other, made each other laugh.

Once the bags got to the waiting area, the Olim had to claim them. Each piece was tagged and plainly marked in black magic marker with their name or other identifying mark. Once they claimed their bags, they then had to be taken down to passport control on the first floor. At this point, each bag had to be handled individually.

We estimated that we loaded twelve tons of luggage on any given sailing—just under a thousand pieces. And each piece was handled five separate times—from the station to the base, the base to the buses, the buses to the port, the port to the ship, and the ship to the cabins. All this was managed by thirty volunteers and a few people from local churches who offered to help. I couldn't believe the excessive amount of work—over and over again. The escalator would have made the job so much easier. We knew it was only the Lord who could pull something of this magnitude off and have no one injured in any way. Roman had worked for a moving company for ten years, but even he had never seen anything like this.

Throughout this horrendous luggage battle, there was also the waiting. After the buses were unloaded, we waited on the second floor

Roman with the human chain of luggage

with the Olim for two or more hours, until passport control opened their doors on the level below. We weren't allowed downstairs until the doors opened, and they seemed purposely slow about doing so. When it was finally okay to go down, there was another wait of about an hour, maybe two, as the Olim and their documents were scrutinized. As we stood with them, they were so grateful, continuing to speak Russian to us, and we did our best to express our hearts to them.

When I considered what it took for them to get to this point, I was again amazed by the Lord's grace and provision. As I said earlier, just gathering each Olim's documents was a feat in itself, especially because many documents, especially for Jews, had been lost after the Second World War. Families were separated, documents destroyed, names changed, and papers burned or lost when people were fleeing for their lives. Yet the Lord brought all this together. "I will go before you and will make the crooked places straight; I will break in pieces the gates of bronze and cut the bars of iron" (Isaiah 45:2).

In the first exodus, events were just as unexplainable. How did the sea part (Exodus 14:21–22)? How did the cloud by day and the fire by night happen (Exodus 13:21)? How was it that their clothes and shoes never wore out (Deuteronomy 29:5)? It was beyond us to figure out. "For my thoughts are not your thoughts, nor are your ways My ways… For as the heavens are higher than the earth, so are My ways higher than your ways, and My thoughts than your thoughts" (Isaiah 55:8–9).

Getting the Olim through passport control was another miraculous feat. It was a grueling process for them. Every piece of paper was checked thoroughly, as well as all monies, valuables, and jewelry, because they were allowed to leave the country with only a certain amount. If anything was going to prevent them from leaving, it was going to happen at passport control. I'd heard stories about rings and jewelry being taken right off of hands and fingers and sentimental treasures being confiscated. The officials were just looking for something to keep these people back. That's why the preparation had to be so meticulous and thorough.

It was standard to have volunteers posted on either side of the passport control area, praying for the families to pass through without incident. Whenever it looked like a family was having difficulty with their documents, word would spread, and that family would be covered in prayer. There was also prayer for the hearts of the customs officials. Each ship had a schedule and had to set sail at a certain time. If the Olim didn't come through by the time the ship was ready to leave, they would be held back. But this rarely happened. Always, at the last minute, anyone who had been detained would come through the doors of passport control, let out a held breath, and be greeted with shouts of "Praise the Lord!" "...He regarded their affliction, when He heard their cry...He also made them to be pitied by all those who carried them away captive" (Psalm 106:44, 46).

Families piled through the other side of the customs hall, the sea of luggage once again rising as we waited for another hour or so before the officials came to open the doors of the building to let us out onto the wharf so that we could board the ship. The Olim's exhaustion was apparent. It had now been more than five hours from the time they had left the bases that morning. Many of the older people, wearied and fatigued, needed a place to sit, but there wasn't any. And the volunteers were getting tired and hungry too. It felt as if we had done a full day's work, but the loading of the ship hadn't even begun. Some of us had brought snacks and sodas, and we passed these around. Handling the luggage made us sweat a lot and get very thirsty.

When the doors to the wharf finally opened, the first to go through were the volunteers who were going on the sailing. They had to surrender their passports to the ship's purser, bring their own luggage to their cabins, and then return to help us load the bags onto the trolleys and gangplank. About eight male volunteers formed the team that would take the bags from the trolleys and carry them up the thirty-two steps onto the ship. From there, another team of about five men and women would take the bags to the cabins. Each bag had a tag on it with the family name and cabin number. As I said, I was assigned to the trolleys. After a few sailings, the leadership nicknamed us "the trolley dollies."

As the Olim came through the doors onto the wharf, two of us would take a single 80–110 pound bag and do the best we could to get it positioned on the trolley so that more bags could go on top of it. It took two of us to push a trolley. It was about 300 feet to the gangplank, and sometimes the wind was so strong, it took all the energy we had to push it straight. We were thankful whenever a sailing day was blessed by calm, sunny weather. When it came to this process, everything mattered—the weather, amenable passport officials, everyone's health, and buses running properly. Rain, and especially snow, made sailings difficult and dangerous. Imagine carrying eighty-pound bags of luggage over the ice-covered steps of the gangplank. Roman once said that he went up and down that gangplank for any given sailing about 150 times.

I could hardly believe we were in the 20th century. I'd watch Roman and the rest of the men come down the gangplank, bend over with their hands on their knees, stretch their backs out, and take deep breaths. It was apparent that this work sapped the very life from them. Yet with all that was going on, there were no mishaps and no injuries. It was truly the grace of God over this work. "He gives power to the weak, and to those who have no might He increases strength" (Isaiah 40:29).

After the luggage was loaded, the Olim began boarding the ship. Some needed assistance walking, some were in wheelchairs. One of the most compelling pictures that is forever etched in my mind is that of the volunteers actually carrying the Olim in their wheelchairs up the steps of the gangplank. Four men were needed for each chair. They'd hoist it up, the dead weight of the person in it trying the grip of the men holding the top and bearing the metal wheels down into the shoulders of the men bracing the bottom. When I saw Roman doing this, knowing it was taking the wind right out of him, I also knew in my heart what he was thinking: that God's people were being taken home and that was all that mattered. I knew how humbled he was to be living out Isaiah 49:22: "...They shall bring your sons in their arms, and your daughters shall be carried on their shoulders."

Many Olim cried as we helped them. They'd never seen anyone take care of them like this. Ebenezer was paying their full way to Israel. Most of their needs were met by us—the tending to of their belongings and their housing, meals, comfort, and care. Most of them had never been given a second look. But God said it in His Word, and here we were living out one prophecy after another. "As a shepherd seeks out his flock...so will I seek out My sheep and deliver them from all the places where they were scattered...and will bring them to their own land" (Ezekiel 34:12–13).

Roman helping carry an Olim in her wheelchair

As the Olim were being registered and checked off the manifest, the team assigned to the ship took their bags to the cabins. Even though I wasn't going on this sailing, I was on this team also, and I cannot adequately express how heavy these bags were. We worked in teams of two, each taking a strap of one bag. Before making it to the cabin, we had to rest often, maybe three times. Many cabins were on the lower and upper levels, so stairs had to be dealt with. The corridors seemed endless and were narrow; the bags seemed twice as wide. So we had to maneuver our bodies in such a way as to carry the luggage long-ways.

At the end of a sailing day, my hands were blistered, my legs bruised from the bags banging against them—it felt like I had been in a football game. Each time we made our way back from taking the bags to the cabin, it seemed there were twice as many more in the receiving area. It was normal to have 300–400 Olim on board any given sailing. With just under a thousand bags, the loading of the ship demanded everything you had, and more. As we got near to the end of loading, the ship provided pizza and soda for the Olim on the back deck. By this time, we could hear the laughter and relief of the Olim and their children in the background as they were enjoying the refreshments. Many had their cameras out, taking pictures of each other. As the ship got ready to leave and the last horn sounded, those of us not sailing made our way off the ship. We gathered on the wharf with the families and friends of those Olim who were sailing and sung a joyous "Bon Voyage." We held a huge Israeli flag to show our love for the Olim and for the nation of Israel. We held hands and repeatedly shouted, "Shalom!"

As the ship made its way out to sea, we sang our favorite Hebrew songs, our hearts bursting with the prophetic gathering of the Lord's people. "For it is good to sing praises to our God…He gathers together the outcasts of Israel" (Psalm 147:1–2).

As hard as the work had been, witnessing this made it all worthwhile. And by making the work more difficult than any of us could have imagined, by keeping it so human, so low, the Lord constantly reminded us that we needed Him more than our own breath. We believed, more than ever, that "He must increase, but I must decrease" (John 3:30).

When the ship became a white speck on the Black Sea, we sighed as one, gathered our belongings, and loaded ourselves into the vans.

Olim waving goodbye from the deck

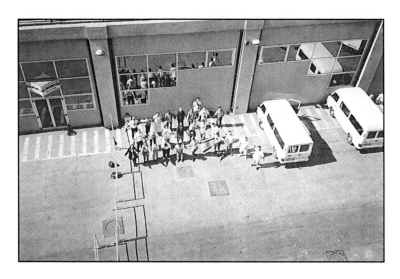

Volunteers singing "Bon Voyage" from port

Roman drove our Lorry, but I could see that he hardly had the strength. I talked with him the whole way to keep him awake.

On the base, we had a quiet dinner. The eight volunteers who had sailed created a palpable absence of family. We were all exhausted, physically and mentally, too tired for conversation. We were even too tired to read the emails that had come in for us while we were at the port. After such grueling work, I worried about Roman eating only the small portion of chicken leg and soup that we were served. But as always, we had no choice. We ate what was in front of us and looked forward to a shower and a cup of instant coffee in our room.

After Roman's shower, I noticed long, red marks, like slashes, on his shoulders and back. He said his shoulders felt like they were on fire. Wincing, I rubbed his back with a cream to help relax his muscles. We never knew how physically demanding this work would be and again thanked God for keeping us in shape.

We sat in bed with our coffees, humbled and spent, wondering about our next assignment. It would be a fishing trip to Kirovograd, a small, countryside area about four hours outside of Odessa. We were to be part of a team of six that would visit Jewish families, tell them about making Aliyah to Israel, and bring humanitarian aid, such as food, clothing, and hygienic items. We had two days to get our belongings together for a two-week trip. And after what we'd just experienced, we didn't even attempt to imagine what lay ahead.

Chapter 8 〜

Learning How to Fish

Behold, I will send for many fishermen…and they shall fish them.
—Jeremiah 16:16

"YOU OKAY, BABE?"

It had taken me awhile to find a spot private enough to pee, and then a few more minutes to relax enough to do it. Concerned by how long I'd been gone, Roman came looking for me. Squatting, I spoke from behind a row of thinning bushes. "Yes, I'm all right, Hon. I'll meet you back in the van."

I'd been warned not to drink too much on the drive, and I didn't think I had. But three and a half hours of pot-holed roads had ping-ponged my bladder to bursting. I longed for the rest stops back home, air conditioning, paved roads, and most of all, toilets and toilet paper. But here it was again—this culture in my face, literally. In this most personal moment, I stared levelly into the resigned brown eyes of a cow.

I rejoined my team, which consisted of six people, three westerners and three Russians—three male, three female. We were on our way to Kirovograd, a city of about 200,000, which once had a significant Jewish population. We were to "fish" there for the next eight days.

Our van was loaded with our luggage, boxes of brochures (written in Russian) explaining Ebenezer's ministry, and about thirty food parcels.

Each parcel contained a box of flour, a bag of sugar, cans of fish, cocoa, cans of milk, bullion, and a few other everyday staples. In the coming days I would see just how much our bringing this humanitarian aid would open the hearts of these people and allow them to hear and believe the promises of their God.

Our ramshackle van plundered along the dusty roads, sandwiched between rolling hills and well-tended farmland. Roman kept pointing out the rich, black earth, saying it reminded him of Poland and how his father always boasted about its fertile soil. The countryside was surprisingly beautiful and stood starkly against the bleakness of our past two weeks in Odessa. It was as if what had been left in God's hands had remained pure and pristine, but what had been touched by man had decayed.

The nearer we drew to the city, the more anxious we became. Where would we be living? What would the conditions be like? Would the families receive us without hostility? Would we stay healthy? We'd heard many stories of volunteers returning from fishing trips sick and depleted. Aside from some broad-brush instructions through a translator, we had no idea what was ahead. We were learning how much of this work involved stepping into the unknown.

When we arrived in Kirovograd, we stopped to visit with a Christian woman our driver knew and who supported Ebenezer's work. We were also to meet a lady named Sophia there. She worked with the repatriation committee in this area, a group of people who helped Jews immigrate to Israel. This group was instrumental in helping the Olim obtain their paperwork, which, as I've said before, was like gold. Sophia had also made arrangements for where we'd be staying and had contacted and scheduled the families we'd be visiting.

An old babushka welcomed us with small sandwiches, tea, and Jell-o. This was a blessing, as we were famished. Through the translator, the woman told us that there was no water at all in her apartment and that she'd be without it for at least ten days. Apparently this was a common problem here, along with unpredictable electrical blackouts.

Sophia arrived as we were eating. With a reassuring, soft-spoken voice, she told us that four of us—Roman and I, plus the translator and another volunteer (both women)—would be staying with a family of four from the local Baptist church. The family consisted of a grandmother, two daughters, and a fifteen-month-old grandson. The husband of the older daughter was in France looking for work and had been gone several months. Poor Roman—he'd be the only male, besides the baby, with six women in what I was sure would be a tiny apartment. The two other volunteers would be staying with another family nearby. I learned that there was rarely a problem finding host families for our fishing teams. People needed money badly, and Ebenezer paid them for room and board for the volunteers.

When we finished our much-appreciated meal, we thanked the woman and prayed for her, her family, and the water situation. Later that day as Roman and I talked, we realized we had the same thought leaving that apartment—how that woman was so hospitable and how she gave out of her nothing to help us in our efforts to find God's people and bring them home.

The apartment building we were to stay in, like most in this country, looked as if it should be condemned. The stories pitched at an angle, as if that side of the foundation had been removed. Some windows were boarded up. Others were covered with plastic sheeting that snapped and billowed in the September wind. Our apartment was on the ninth floor. Not surprisingly, the electricity was out. Without the lift or lights, we literally had to watch our step. I was behind Roman, who led the way, carrying both our bags. More than once he paused on a stairwell and looked back, saying things like: "It's sturdier to the left." "Avoid the middle." "A few steps almost collapsed on me." Or, "The sixth step is missing," and we'd have to count. There were tiny windows on every other stairwell, all painted shut. The air was stifling and smelled like old, wet wool. About half way up, my stomach roiled. Roman knew. "We're almost there, Babe."

Our translator found the apartment and knocked on the splintering door. The three of us were behind her, our rhythmic panting the only sound on the narrow landing. We were greeted by a small, moon-faced woman with freckled skin. When she saw us, her blue eyes lit like sparklers. I knew this must be the grandmother, as she had the customary babushka kerchief tied snugly behind her head. But she was much younger than I expected, I guessed no more than fifty.

She led us into a narrow hallway, wiping her hands on a frayed, food-stained apron tied around her waist. We slipped off our shoes, which we were told beforehand to do out of respect. The translator began speaking in Russian. I knew she was explaining the logistics of our stay to the grandmother—that Ebenezer would pay her for housing us and for food for everyone for the time we'd be with her. The babushka's dire need for money needed no translation. She was rapt, her little hands clasped to her chest.

After they talked, we were led into a small living room. Then we were shown the two, even smaller, bedrooms. This apartment made our modest home back in the states seem palatial. How in the world were seven adults and a baby going to live here for two weeks?

The living room was about ten by fifteen. There was a worn green sofa, a faded orange recliner, and a small television, which sat on a three-legged stool and had what looked like an elongated coat hanger stuck in a broken antenna hole. One wall was almost completely covered with a surprisingly beautiful, expensive-looking Persian rug. We would come to see this type of unexpected wall covering in almost every home we visited.

The babushka began speaking animatedly in Russian, pointing to the bedrooms, to Roman and me, and then to her two daughters, who had joined us. I knew she was talking about sleeping arrangements. The translator told us that because we were a married couple, Roman and I would sleep on the pull-out couch in the living room. There were folding doors that we could close at night. We were thankful, as if we'd been given the master suite. The translator and the other volunteer would take the small bedroom in the back and share a bed. This was where the babushka and one daughter usually slept. During our stay, the four of them—the babushka, her two daughters, and the baby—would sleep in the even smaller second bedroom. Later I realized that the mother and two daughters slept on the floor, the baby in his crib.

After these arrangements were explained, the translator told us about the water situation. Once again, we realized what we had taken for granted back home. There was cold, running water from 6 P.M. until midnight only and no hot water at all. So water needed to be stored in pots for the morning and for flushing toilets. Also, the water had to be

Our host family in Kirovograd

boiled before we used it for washing. There was a small basin, the size of a dishpan, in the bathroom that we were to use for washing. There would be no showers for our entire stay, just sponge or "G.I. baths," as they were referred to in the army. The babushka assured us that she'd have pots ready for us on the stove each morning and evening.

We'd been traveling since dawn. At this point I was so drained I felt like I didn't even have that mustard seed of faith to move the mountain before us (Luke 17:6). But I was too tired to worry about it. I didn't care if the water was ice cold. All I wanted to do was brush my teeth and wash my face.

It was well into evening, and Roman and I had to wait our turn for the bathroom. Once we washed up, we settled into our "suite," thanking the Lord for providing for us. We thanked Him for the sacrifice of these people. They were so used to inconvenience, to living in the shadow of hardship. But we needed to get some sleep, to block everything out of our minds for the night. We knew a good night's rest was crucial.

We quietly closed the flimsy folding doors to the living room. Then we folded the small table that was used for meals and propped it against the wall to make room for the pull-out couch. The mattress had been made with a worn sheet and two thin blankets. We quickly changed into our sleeping clothes, and I grabbed my Bible for some quick encouragement before sleep. I set our travel alarm clock for 7 A.M. and then read this verse from Isaiah 41:10 to Roman before settling into the lumpy mattress: "So do not fear, for I am with you; do not be dismayed, for I am your God. I will strengthen you and help you; I will uphold you with my righteous hand."

First Day of Fishing

The next morning we quickly grabbed our clothes, got dressed, folded the bed back into the couch, and readied the table and chairs for the breakfast meal. This would be our daily ritual for the next nine days. Then we opened the doors to the living room and waited for our turn in the bathroom. Roman was a gentleman, letting all the ladies go before him. True to her word, the babushka had two large pots of

Kirovograd fishing team (Roman and I are second and third from the left)

heated water on the stove, which unfortunately were cool by the time Roman's turn came around.

The babushka made us a lovely breakfast of sausage, kasha (a type of porridge), bread, and tea. As we finished, the other two volunteers met us in the apartment. We gathered in the living room and prayed for the Lord's direction and favor to be with us as we visited the Jewish families. We had planned to try and visit four homes a day. All the families had been contacted beforehand by Ebenezer so that they would be expecting us.

We made our way down the nine flights of stairs much more easily than we'd made our way up them the day before. Though the lift was working, we decided not to chance it. The electricity was so unpredictable; we didn't want to get stuck if it went out. It was amazing what a good night's rest and some hot food does for the spirit. All in all, we felt healthy and at peace and that the Lord was with us.

We took our spots in the van and headed for the first family. All we had learned over the last few years about the Lord's people began to fill me—how they are "the apple of His eye" (Deuteronomy 32:10) and how He dispersed them but promised in Isaiah 54:7 to bring them back: "For a mere moment I have forsaken you, but with great mercies I will gather you." Now we would be able to directly share some of this truth with them. How would we do this? Would the translator be able to communicate His heart through us? Would His people even understand? Would we really be equipped to do this? At that moment I realized something fantastic that smothered every one of those questions with a palpable reassurance, as if God Himself were driving the van. This first day of our fishing trip was Yom Kippur—the holiest of Jewish holidays!

Our first stop was the apartment of an elderly lady named Nina. As she led us inside, we took off our shoes and made our way to the small living area. It was much like "our" apartment—small and simple, with the same type of rug on the living room wall. She seemed to have no more than "our" family did and was obviously happy to have us. She greeted us with a big smile, wide-eyed at seeing all of us from different nations.

As would come to be the procedure with all the families we'd visit, the translator first shared about what Ebenezer's mission was, where we were all from, and that God had put it on our hearts to come here to help them return to Israel. Then she explained the logistics of the ship, the documents required to leave the country, and the assistance Ebenezer offered in obtaining their documents.

Nina told us that she had actually begun the process about two years before with Sophia. The paperwork, as always, was the biggest obstacle, and was still being worked on. As Nina was already in the process of making Aliyah, there wasn't much to be done here. But it was a good run-through. It was as if the Lord knew what we needed and that we would be more comfortable with having had a training ground. We prayed with her, left a food parcel, and made our way to the second family.

An elderly lady named Henrietta graciously invited us into a carbon copy of Nina's apartment. Amazingly, we found out through our translator that Henrietta is born again and believes in Yeshua (the Hebrew term for Jesus) as her Messiah! This was about as common here as dependable running water and electricity. She shared how she and her family had escaped from the Nazis. While they were on the run, her mother had dropped all their documents in a puddle. The ink ran on Henrietta's birth certificate, making it hard to prove that she was of Jewish heritage.

I tried to imagine what it must have been like for her and her family. As I had been while waiting at the train stations for the Olim, I was brought back to the realization that this was the land where so much devastation had been wrought on the Jewish people. We were hearing firsthand what I'd only read about in history books.

Henrietta said that she wanted to go to Israel. Through our translator, we told her that Ebenezer would help her obtain her documents. She served us tea and biscuits and pastries she had baked for Rosh Hashanah a few weeks before. She was so moved by our visit that she told the translator that she wanted to pray for *us* before we left. What an unexpected gift! We went there to bless her, and she blessed us!

Henrietta's apartment

Our third stop was to visit a very elderly lady who lived with her daughter. Once again, we were graciously invited to come inside. I was stunned by how readily, and with such trust, we were received by these people. True, they had been expecting us. But within the confines of the regulation and oppression that framed their lives, their hospitality was a heartwarming confirmation that the Lord was, indeed, going before us.

After the translator gave our introductions and explained what Ebenezer's mission was, it was clear that the daughter was open to leaving. But from the mother's solemnity, it was equally clear that she wasn't. And the daughter would not go to Israel without her mother. The translator suggested that, for now, we should pray and then make a return trip. So we prayed with them for the release of their documents and silently that God would gently change the mother's heart.

The fourth and last stop before lunch was to be at Sophia's apartment. She had invited about a dozen people to meet us there. Her apartment was a bit larger than the others, and it was a good thing too. There were about fifteen or twenty people gathered in her living room. Some were standing, some were sitting, and others were leaning against the walls.

Sophia spoke in Russian as the translator spoke to us in English. Sophia told them about Ebenezer and making Aliyah to Israel, mainly about the documents and logistics. Then it was our turn to speak about the spiritual side. So right from the Scriptures, Roman shared about Ebenezer's "Operation Exodus," about the return of the Lord's people to their homeland. He told them, through the prophet Isaiah's words, how their God had called us, the nations, to help them make this return and to accompany them on the ship all the way to Haifa. "Behold, I will lift My hand in an oath to the nations…They shall bring your sons in their arms, and your daughters shall be carried on their shoulders" (Isaiah 49:22).

Roman's voice, deep and resonant, continued to echo the Psalms, verses from Isaiah, Jeremiah, and Zechariah. Even before the words were translated, I could see the effect that this handsome, strong American reverently reading from his Bible had on the room. Faces became hopeful and expectant. Eyes blinked and widened. And then, as they heard the words in their own language, as they listened to their very own God for the first time, I saw the first of many of God's promises made manifest: "I will give you a new heart and put a new spirit within you" (Ezekiel 36:26). Questioning and skeptical expressions transformed into longing. Eyes dimmed for decades by lies and despair cleared and shone. The magnitude of God's love for His people and the promise of His truth were being brought to bear on His people's hearts as Roman continued, "For I will take you from among the nations, gather you out of all countries, and bring you into your own land" (Ezekiel 36:24).

I sat there in awe. Who was I to be in the midst of something so profound and prophetic? I possessed nothing in myself to warrant it, to have been chosen for "such a time as this" (Esther 4:14). It reminded me, and not for the first time, of the words of Jesus as he spoke to His disciples: "...for without Me, you can do nothing" (John 15:5). As I watched, I began to see firsthand the power of God's Word at work—that it truly does "accomplish what I please, and it shall prosper in the thing for which I sent it" (Isaiah 55:11) and that it truly "is living and powerful, and sharper than any two-edged sword, piercing even to the division of soul and spirit, and of joints and marrow" (Hebrews 4:12).

When Roman was finished, all the Olim walked over to the table where the Ebenezer brochures had been stacked and began reading them. You could visibly see the blessing being manifested. You could see the effect this visit was having on them. They seemed startled by the love, concern, and commitment we had for them, and by the measure of faith we had on their behalf to believe that whatever documents and paperwork, whatever legalities lay in their path, God would make a way for them. The fact that we came from all corners of the earth just for them was in itself a motivating factor.

Before we left, we prayed for the group. We prayed that their hearts would be open to the call of their God and that His favor would rest on those deciding to make Aliyah so that all of the logistics and paperwork would fall into place. As we were leaving, the Olim were lining up, brochures in hand, waiting for their turn to ask the translator questions.

As we made our way back to the apartment for lunch, we talked about this crescendo visit of the day. We discussed how God, like a father

Olim listening to Roman speak about Aliyah

teaching a child to ride a bicycle, had used the first three visits to steady us. And then, when He knew we were ready, He let go.

It was about noon at this point. We had made plans with the babushka to return to the flat each day for lunch between 12:30 and 1:00 P.M., so we headed back. I was exhausted, but not so much physically as spiritually. All the walking I had done for so many years had kept me in shape. It was as if the Lord had been preparing me for this work of walking, waiting, and climbing stairs. But spiritually, there was no way I could have been prepared and no way to know how I'd feel when face to face with the living Word of God, when living out holy prophecy in the style of the apostles. It simply rendered me speechless.

The aromas from the babushka's creative hand in the kitchen reeled us up those nine flights of stairs like a fishing lure. It continued to amaze me how she whipped together these hearty meals—three a day for seven people—in this tiny kitchen. And she did it with no running water and no fancy appliances—just the most basic food. But it was always wonderful. Roman, especially, savored each meal. It was usually soup, but different every day. She made a magnificent broth and then added beef or chicken, noodles or potatoes, and vegetables. And the bread was homemade and warm. Roman was raised on these kinds of staples when he lived in the camps in Germany, so it helped him to feel comfortable in this culture.

Over lunch we reviewed everything we had done that morning, continually commenting on how gracious and welcoming the Jewish people were to us. Because it was Yom Kippur and because we had already made four visits, we decided to take the rest of the day off. We were still recuperating a bit from the day of traveling and settling in, and we needed time to digest our first day.

As evening came and supper was finished, the routine that would be repeated for the upcoming eight days began. At six o'clock, the cold water began running (it would stop at midnight), and the babushka put two huge pots of water on the stove for us. They took nearly an hour to boil. We each bathed as best we could, taking turns in the bathroom with a dishpan of hot water.

This was close living as I'd never been in before. But I was surprised (though I shouldn't have been) at how the Lord was over it all. Everyone looked out for the next person. Everyone was considerate. There was no tension or striving. Roman managed among all the women, allowing the Lord to be his companion.

Roman and I felt privileged to be in our little suite, being able to close the doors at night and having a measure of solitude and privacy. Just behind the wall of our bed was the babushka with her two daughters sleeping on the floor. I thought about them many times as I slept on the couch they had given up for us and remembered the bedroom they had given to the other women. Again, here were these people giving out of their nothing.

Second Day of Fishing

Lumpy mattress and all, Roman and I slept soundly, even more so than the previous night. We woke refreshed and immediately folded the couch and opened the table for the morning meal. As this was our second day in the apartment, the morning bathroom ritual became a little more palatable than the day before. The babushka, bless her, had the two large pots ready and hot on the stove. The toilet was in a separate space with a door, as were the tub and sink, which made it a bit easier and more efficient for all of us.

We had no particular schedule with the bathroom, we just watched for which spot was free. For convenience, we usually kept a large pail of water next to the toilet for flushing and extra water in the tub. We had to try to remember to make sure the toilet was full of clean water after we used it, or it would be more work for the next person who had to use the bathroom. And it could be embarrassing for the previous person. This problem was so unbelievable to me. We were being exposed to a culture that most of us knew only from history books or from hazy recollections of our grand or great-grandparents. Day by day, this work stretched and pulled at the privileged and pampered lifestyle we had grown so accustomed to.

After another warm and hearty breakfast lovingly prepared by the babushka, we got ready for our next day of fishing. The other two men from the team met us at the apartment, and we prayed for the Lord to be over all that we'd be doing for and with His people that day.

Our first visit was to a family of four—father, mother, daughter, and granddaughter. Again, we were graciously received and invited into their home. The translator shared the practical side of Ebenezer's ministry, explaining the need for documents and the logistics of the sailing. Then the father told her that he had promised to take his family to Israel, a promise he said he would not break. This was a big encouragement for us, of course. But he said that he was worried about the difficulty of selling their apartment. In addition, his wife needed to have some sort of surgery.

We read passages of Scripture to them, which were then translated. I cannot describe what this felt like. Other than to say: what could be more life-affirming than to speak destiny to God's own people through their own Word from the Old Testament? It created a bridge between us and them, Gentile and Jew, something greater than any person, organization, ministry, or government.

We prayed for the family and left them a food parcel, for which they were very appreciative. We also left some brochures and the phone numbers of all the contacts who could help them, both in selling their apartment and in finding medical help. This need for proper medical care was something I'd see repeatedly as our time went on.

Our second stop was to see a mother and her thirty-two-year-old son. Their apartment was eight flights up, and again, the lift wasn't working. We watched for broken steps and cracked cement as we made our way, using a small flashlight that I'd had the presence of mind to take along.

The mother, an obese lady, met us at the door with a smile. She welcomed us inside, her very movements seemingly a chore. When the translator finished sharing about the ministry, we, through her, shared how the Lord had called us from all the nations to find His people and help to bring them home on the ship. She then told us about her need for medical attention. When we explained that wonderful medical care was available to her in Israel, she said she'd be willing to go if her son was. But he was a truck driver and at work, so we said we'd return another time and speak with him. We read Scripture to her, left a food parcel, and then made our way to the next family.

In the van, I thought about this woman and how obviously hard it was for her to even move around. I wondered if she ever got any fresh air. With the lift not working, it would be impossible for her to manage the eight flights of stairs. And if she did get down in the lift and then it went out, she'd be stranded. And what if she got stuck in the lift when the power went out? It was so small and cramped, how would she be able to stand it? As we got close to the next stop, I had to let all of this go and prepare myself for the next family. It seemed that so much of the daily life here lacked the basic necessities and comforts we were used to back home. These people were leaving such impressions on my heart, and I didn't yet know how to put them in the Lord's hands. So I had to force myself to stop thinking about it and just concentrate on what was before me.

The next family was a husband and wife. After the translator shared the work of Ebenezer and explained how and why we were all there, the husband informed her that he was an atheist, saying that he'd been hurt many years ago in the synagogue by a rabbi. Although we couldn't understand the words when he spoke them, his anger needed no translation. He said he preferred to die in Ukraine.

We watched and listened as the translator patiently spoke with him. For the most part, people here came from the same level of society, where no one had any more than anyone else. They knew how to talk to each other, and the husband listened and seemed to understand. Then Roman shared the Scripture references to Aliyah with him: "Behold, I will send for many fishermen...and they shall fish them; and afterward I will send for many hunters, and they shall hunt them from every mountain and every hill, and out of the holes of the rocks" (Jeremiah 16:16). "Up, up! Flee from the land of the north...for I have spread you abroad like the four winds of heaven...Up, Zion! Escape, you who dwell with the daughter of Babylon" (Zechariah 2:6–7). Then we prayed with the man and his wife and shared the need for him to forgive the rabbi.

These visits usually lasted about an hour, but we'd been with the man and his wife for almost two and needed to get on to our next family. It seemed each family had its own particular obstacle that discouraged them or made it seem next to impossible for them to leave. As with the family that morning, selling their flats was a major concern for many. But we had to trust the Lord. These were His people, and as we moved in faith in Him, He would have to make "a way in the sea and a path through the mighty waters" (Isaiah 43:16). Never before was I faced with such a challenge to trust in Him. As each day passed and as each family was visited, this level of trust in all that He could do was beginning to take hold of my heart as nothing else ever had.

Like all the others, the woman at our next stop graciously invited us into her home. She listened intently as the translator explained the practical side of Ebenezer's work, intermittently asking questions. We noticed that she'd get weepy from time to time, which was something we hadn't experienced with the other families. Then the translator explained that this woman's only son had died nine years ago from a massive heart attack.

As the translator explained this, the woman began to grieve uncontrollably. One of our team members, Elaine, rushed to the woman's side and held her. Elaine's twelve-year-old daughter had been struck by a car and died only a few years before. Here was God, again showing up for His people. "'Comfort, yes, comfort My people!' says your God. 'Speak comfort to Jerusalem'" (Isaiah 40:1–2). As Elaine held this woman, the Lord bathed her in His Word through Roman's reading of Scripture. By the time we left, the Lord's healing hand was apparent over this woman's life. He showed us how "He heals the brokenhearted and binds up their wounds" (Psalm 147:3). Again and again, right before our eyes, Scripture came alive.

To be in these homes with the Bible wide open, sharing prophetic Scripture with the very people the words were written for was an experience that will forever be etched in our hearts. Though they were not believers in Jesus and we were not permitted to evangelize (just to "bring His people home"), these were God's people. I watched their faces as Roman read to them, and I could see that though they'd never heard any of this before, it was making an impression. I saw with my own eyes truth in the making, the Word of God that would undergird this work from beginning to end. "So shall my word be that goes forth from My mouth; it shall not return to Me void, but it shall accomplish what I please, and it shall prosper in the thing for which I sent it" (Isaiah 55:11). We believed the Lord for every family we visited. We were merely planters of the seed. Only God could water and cultivate it.

Elaine and the team comforting the grieving woman

We'd done enough for the day and headed back to our apartment for some food, fellowship, and rest. How the babushka organized everything for us continued to amaze me. In her tiny kitchen, with her little stove and sink, no running water until 6 at night, she prepared three feast-like meals every day, in addition to watching a fifteen-month-old baby.

We all looked forward to time around the table at supper. After listening to the stories firsthand from the mouths of the Lord's people, we needed to empty our hearts with one another. We talked about the day, exchanged thoughts and ideas, and went over anything we felt we could have shared more about or done better with.

The babushka gave us our time together and then, toward the end of our meal, she'd sit with us. Like most people here, it was clear she'd had a hard life. The language barrier made it difficult for us to understand most of what she said, and the translator was too tired from a whole day of translating to do much more. But smiles, hugs, and laughter sometimes communicate better than words.

After supper, we again went through our evening routine with our little dishpans of hot water. We had already had a few days without a shower, but it didn't seem so bad. I was getting used to this, learning that this kind of living was hard but not impossible. I was learning to live without convenience or comfort, just with necessity. There was always such peace in the apartment that I knew the Lord was with us. And that was all that mattered to me.

Third Day of Fishing

The next morning when I went into the kitchen to get my portion of hot water, I was met by the baby playing on the floor with a bowl and spoon. He gave me the biggest smile as I said good morning in the best Russian I knew. He seemed very obedient, very happy with his makeshift toy. There were no other toys around, and my thoughts rushed back to all the children at home with their toys, gadgets, and books. While many children in the States have too much, my heart ached for this little boy to have the books and toys that sharpen learning and stimulate coordination.

There was no level of society there that was untouched by the necessity for more help. Need was a systemic thing, and every time I saw it, my heart wanted to fix it. But as the days went on, the Lord began to show me that I wasn't there to do that.

After breakfast, the other two volunteers met with us at the apartment to pray. We asked the Lord to go before us and to open the hearts and minds of His people to His living Word. We asked for His protection, His heart, His words, His mercy. He was all we had to lean on.

Our first stop was the flat of two very elderly women. They met us with smiles, and walking slowly, they directed us into their small living space. It had just the bare necessities—a couch against the wall, a few old chairs, and a bed in the corner.

The translator introduced us all, explaining where we were from. After she told them about Ebenezer and about making Aliyah, she asked them a few questions. We found out one lady was eighty-six and the other was ninety. The younger took care of the older woman, who seemed especially slow and tired. As Jews living in the former Soviet Union during this century, I could only imagine what they had seen in their lifetimes. And then I thought that maybe it was the Lord's mercy that we couldn't speak their language, maybe it was His mercy that we didn't know what they had endured. Maybe our hearts were not strong enough.

As we spoke with them through the translator, the younger one seemed anxious to leave, but the older one didn't want to go. We shared scriptures with them, prayed, and left a good-sized food parcel. I thought that as old as they were, it would be nothing less than a miracle for the Lord to move in their hearts.

At the next flat we were greeted by another elderly, very hospitable woman. Her apartment was much like the others: simple, blasé, plain. This was so unlike back home. Even if homes looked the same on the outside, the insides were all different, reflecting the owners' personalities. But this society was all the same—lifeless, without any personal expression.

After the usual introductions, the translator spoke with this lady for a long time. Most of this woman's relatives were killed during the pogroms and during the war. They were all buried in Ukraine, and she

86-and 90-year-old Ladies

wanted to be buried with them. She had no desire to leave for Israel. We had been told on the base that the people in Ukraine have an unusual bond with the dead and that they treasure their family's graves. They visit gravesites often and even eat while visiting there, making it more of a social occasion, as macabre as that sounds. But this was the first time I had seen this "love for the dead" firsthand. It's like some sort of stronghold, some sort of demonic belief that if they leave the country they will be abandoning their family.

This was the first time I and another volunteer sensed the need to pray in the Spirit and the need for the Holy Spirit to show us what to do. The Lord pointed us to Jeremiah and Zechariah, and we read the Scriptures out loud to her. "But I will gather the remnant of My flock out of all countries where I have driven them, and bring them back to their folds" (Jeremiah 23:3). We shared that in her midst sat the nations of the world who came across oceans and lands just to deliver the Word of the Lord to her. We also told her that this might be her only opportunity to heed the Word being shared with her, because the persecution of Jews was rising in this land and the Lord wanted to save her from it. "Up! Up! Flee from the land of the north" (Zechariah 2:6).

I imagined what it must have been like only sixty years ago. I wondered how many were warned then of the upcoming atrocities and how many took heed. This lady had been a nurse for forty-one years and had served with the frontline troops during World War II. How did she ever get through all that?

But still, I could understand the struggle that must have been going on inside of her. Her age alone was a factor. How do you just pick up and leave your country after seventy-six years of living there? It was easier for the young, who had their whole lives ahead of them, to make Aliyah. But for the very old? The number of elderly that the Lord had us visit was overwhelming. Out of their mouths were coming firsthand stories of atrocities and suffering portrayed only in movies or on the History Channel back home. But this was where the Holy Spirit moved. "Not by might, nor by power, but by My Spirit, says the Lord of hosts" (Zechariah 4:6). Every question I asked had only one answer: God. Only God alone can do this.

Before saying our goodbyes, we prayed with this woman and knew we were leaving her in the trustworthy hands of the Lord. We gave her a good-sized food parcel and lots of hugs and kisses. She startled us with her appreciation by repeatedly kissing our hands and arms. I kept telling her, through the translator, that it was her God who had come to share His love and provision. He was the one to give thanks to, the one who loved her beyond measure.

Each family we visited and each person's story slowly but steadily drained us. And we knew we had only so much to give. I had never had to rely totally on the Lord for His living grace in such a measure. Many times I thought of the words of Jesus as he spoke with the woman at the well: "…whoever drinks of the water that I shall give him will never thirst. But the water that I shall give him will become in him a fountain of water springing up into everlasting life" (John 4:14). We were living this truth, drawing on His Word as we spoke it to His people, feeling it well up and quench our spirits.

Privileged and handpicked, we had been drawn into an unimaginable situation by an unexplainable pull. I had never known this kind of depth in God, this kind of faith, trust, and total dependence. What had I been living all the years before? Was it preparation for "such a time as this" (Esther 4:14)? Again and again, I'd think of what Job said: "I have heard of You by the hearing of the ear, but now my eye sees You" (Job 42:5).

Our third visit was to another elderly lady. From looking at the flat, it was obvious she lived on the bare minimum, and I guessed her pension must be next to nothing. She listened as the translator gave the information about the work of Ebenezer. Then she spoke with the translator, who explained her situation to us. The woman was eighty-four and widowed. She and her husband had been bakers until he became an invalid. She had taken care of him until he passed away.

We shared with her how the Lord had allowed her to live this long for the living hope that He would return her to the land of her forefathers, that she was alive in this day to see the faithfulness of her God, and that He was touching her through us. In her eyes and through her heart we could see her readiness to leave. I sat amazed at His great love. We were witnessing a miracle—the heart of this eighty-four-year-old yielding itself willingly to the Savior's grace. Again, it was, "Not by might, nor by power, but by My Spirit, says the Lord of hosts" (Zechariah 4:6).

The experience was beyond what I can express here, being in the middle of a Second Exodus and actually being the bearers of the Word of the Lord to His own people. At the same time, the Lord, through all the circumstances and difficulties, kept our hearts from becoming puffed up with our own pride. It was a balance that only He, through the remembrance of His Word, could bring. "Your word I have hidden in my heart, that I might not sin against You" (Psalm 119:11).

We prayed with this lady, left a food parcel and brochures, and encouraged her to contact us for any help she needed. As these people made decisions to leave, there were obstacles at every turn. But Ebenezer would do everything and anything to see them safely planted in the land of Israel.

It was not an easy thing to shake the dust off from one flat and go right to another. The fact that these apartments were not always easy to find and that we'd often get lost was actually a blessing. We all needed the time between visits to gather our thoughts and strengthen ourselves in the Lord. Sometimes we'd ask the translator to teach us a few Russian phrases to speak to the people, and this was always a laugh. Our western accents flowed clumsily through this rough language, and that lifted some of the heaviness.

Our next stop was to visit another lady, a bit younger, maybe in her sixties. After introductions by the translator, she told us that this woman had a son living in Israel. She said that he kept in touch with her and often wrote about the hot climate. The woman said she didn't want to go to Israel because of the heat. These people had lived in the cold, harsh climate of Russia for so long that they had no perspective of anything better. We found this with many of the elderly—they were more afraid of the heat in Israel than they were of the anti-Semitism that was on the rise in this nation. We silently prayed for the Lord to remove the fear from her heart of Israel's hot weather and to replace it with a longing for her green and lush land.

We prayed comfort, love, and encouragement over her, said our goodbyes, and left our usual food parcel. It had been a long morning, and we needed some food and rest. As we made our way back to our apartment in the van, all of us were quiet, pensive. I knew we were thinking of warm bread and hot soup.

The table had already been set, and we gathered around the "banquet" that had been prepared. How much we appreciated this babushka. How faithful she was. She seemed to make so much from nothing. It was exhausting to think about how she managed every day for all of us. The food on the base seemed like rations compared with the home cooking we were eating here.

After we ate, we talked with one another, sharing about our families back home. This was very healthy for us, as we missed our families terribly. And here we couldn't call or email at all. Even on the base, calls home were infrequent, as they were astronomically expensive. Most of the volunteers waited until they sailed to Israel and made calls from there. For us, that would only be a week or so away.

As long as the mornings seemed, the afternoons raced by. Once we'd had lunch, visited with each other, and talked and rested, evening was upon us. We'd have our usual, lovingly-prepared, "elegant" meal and then start in on our bathroom routine. By now, we had it down pat. And it actually didn't seem so bad.

Fourth Day of Fishing

Refreshed and renewed by a good night's sleep, we were all ready for a new day. When I woke, I smelled breakfast, heard the babushka rustling about, and listened to the baby playing in the kitchen. This tiny apartment, this close living was unexpectedly beginning to feel like home.

After breakfast, we had our usual prayer meeting with the other two volunteers, asking the Lord for his covering as we carried out His work. We were to make only one stop this morning, as Sophia had arranged for us to meet several Jewish families at a local school in the afternoon.

The woman we visited was overjoyed to see us, excitement obvious in her expression. The translator told us that she was in the process of making Aliyah already and that her paperwork was in process. She felt special because we came to her home, as Sophia had been the only one to visit her. She made us some chai (tea) and set out little cakes and cookies.

We prayed for all her documents to be released and for protection and comfort to be released upon her. We left her with a food parcel and returned to the flat for lunch before heading to the school.

The school building, like most buildings we had seen, looked like a cement slab. There was no grass, no flowers or bushes, just dirt packed down by a herd of footprints. It seemed like such a depressing learning environment. Inside was even worse.

The auditorium where our meeting was to be held was enormous and dimly lit. I looked up at the cracked and paint-chipped ceiling to find only about a third of the lights working. There was a stage at the front of the room, its floor warped to the point that it pitched at about a thirty-degree angle. When I took my seat in the front, the entire row slid back about a foot, and I nearly fell to the floor. The bolts that held the seats to the floor were missing. The first thing I thought of was the children and how easily they could get hurt. Apparently there was no maintenance at all on these buildings. I knew the area was depressed and poverty-stricken, but I didn't expect the schools to be in as horrific shape as the flats were. By U.S. standards, I was sure this building would be condemned.

People began filing in, and when the group reached about fifteen, Sophia opened the meeting. As she shared about the work of Ebenezer, I could only imagine that all of these people wanted more for their families and children than the conditions and situations they found themselves in. Many had no future here and were stuck in a cycle of poverty and hopelessness. Though life in Israel wasn't easy, at least there would be opportunity to learn and advance in areas that were not available in Ukraine. And they'd be able to get much-needed medical attention.

When Sophia was finished, she asked Roman to share about the spiritual side of Ebenezer's work. First he told of his own experience and of how God had called him from America to help them. He shared that he had left his country and his family, his job and his security to do this work. He told them that the Lord, their God, the God of Abraham,

Isaac, and Jacob, was calling them out of their country as well: "The Lord your God will…have compassion on you, and gather you again from all the nations where the Lord your God has scattered you…He will bring you… to the land which your fathers possessed, and you shall possess it" (Deuteronomy 30:3–5). Roman explained that He is a faithful God and that He would care for them through this transition and be with them every step of the way. Their only job was to trust Him. "Fear not, for I have redeemed you…When you pass through the waters, I will be with you…When you walk through the fire, you shall not be burned… Fear not, for I am with you" (Isaiah 43:1–2, 5).

When Roman finished, the neglected auditorium thundered with applause, like a forsaken heart quickened by newfound hope. We invited each person to come forward to receive a food parcel. As they did, we hugged them and distributed the fliers and brochures from Ebenezer. All the information they needed to begin Aliyah was explained in these materials.

By this point, I needed a bathroom badly and made my way to the girls' bathroom down the hall. *Not again!* It was as if I were back in that bathroom in the Odessa airport. I walked in and then right out. As I was telling the translator how horrible the bathroom was, the principal of the school happened to be next to us. He proudly offered the teachers' bathroom at the other end of the hall. Hopeful, I headed toward it and ran into Roman, who had just used the men's bathroom. I should have listened to his warning.

The broken floor and chipped walls didn't bother me. But when I saw that the toilet was nothing more than a stench-filled hole in the ground, I just couldn't bring myself to use it. This planted a real fear in me any time I had to use a bathroom outside of our flat.

I don't know how I made it through the long ride back to the apartment, but I did. When we arrived, I made a bee line to the clean, private little room that housed our toilet. Five days ago I had been anxious at the thought of living like this. But now, so relieved, I thankfully picked up the bucket of water beside the toilet and, praising the Lord, emptied it into the bowl.

Supper was, once again, the highlight of our (especially Roman's) day. Enjoying another of the babushka's miraculous feasts, we relaxed and reviewed the day, encouraged by both of our meetings. By now, we had the evening routine down pat. When supper was finished, everyone pitched in to clear the table and then took turns washing the dishes with water heated on the stove. Then we all helped with filling buckets and pots for the toilet, and everyone took a turn in the bathroom. Amazingly, there was no tension, no strife, no one hurrying anyone else or seeming impatient.

Fifth Day of Fishing

Each morning I woke from a sounder sleep than the night before. This had to be of the Lord, because each day of fishing was becoming increasingly more taxing on my mind and spirit.

We had our usual prayer meeting before leaving the flat. It was a simple time, as we were simple people, none of us with any special training to do what we were doing. Roman and I were the oldest of the group, which was sometimes awkward. The three Russians on our team were in their twenties, young enough to have been our children. As the days went on, though we didn't understand the language, we saw arguments that would create an atmosphere of tension. Our instinct as their elders and as parents was to intervene and mediate. But the language barrier prevented that, so we just turned it over to the Lord, and He always smoothed things out. "The crooked roads shall be made straight and the rough ways smooth" (Luke 3:5).

Our first stop was at the home of yet another very elderly couple. The wife had been expecting us and eagerly invited us in. I got the impression that so many of these people never had visitors outside of their immediate families. This woman seemed as if she were bursting to talk to someone.

Her husband was in the living room. He was stout and big-chested, with the countenance of a World War II veteran. The translator explained the work of Ebenezer, who we all were, and why we had come. After we introduced ourselves, she spoke through the translator that she felt so special and privileged to have people from other countries come to her meager little apartment. And meager it was, even more so than the others we'd visited. This couple sadly represented the poor, old people of

Ukraine, their drawn, road-mapped faces a testament to a life of struggle and toil. As I looked around, lack glared from every corner. We were told through the translator that they had been eating bread and pepper mash for breakfast, and now they were down to the very end of all their food. What a miracle it was that we had come with a food parcel.

Roman began to share the scriptures about God's call for them to return to the land of their ancestors. The wife was captivated, but the husband seemed distant and disinterested. We then learned that he was left partially deaf from the war. When Roman was finished, the woman grabbed her husband's head, turned his ear toward her mouth, and nearly screamed into his ear, relaying in Russian what Roman had spoken through the translator.

Almost instantly, his eyes filled with tears. As they streamed down his wrinkled face, my own eyes began to sting. This was the heart of Aliyah. This is the work we came to do—to breathe life into a land of dry bones. "O dry bones, hear the word of the Lord...I will cause breath to enter into you, and you shall live" (Ezekiel 37:4–5). And again, Isaiah 55:11 was manifest: "So shall My word be that goes forth from My mouth; it shall not return to Me void, but it shall accomplish what I please, and it shall prosper in the thing for which I sent it."

We prayed that they would spend the rest of their years in their rightful home, the land of Israel. We left two food parcels with them. The woman was so grateful that she grabbed our hands, kissing them over and over again. This was the second time this had happened. As with the other woman, I kept telling her that this was her God reaching out to her, that we were only His messengers. We felt like Peter in the book of Acts, when he visited Cornelius. "As Peter was coming in, Cornelius met him and fell down at his feet and worshiped him. But Peter lifted him up, saying, 'Stand up; I myself am also a man'" (Acts 10:25–26).

Our next stop was an old house that looked more like a shanty in the middle of a junkyard. We were met by an elderly, disheveled man who lived alone. He was unshaven, his clothes worn and dirty. The inside was an extension of the outside. The small house was crowded with pieces of car parts, toilets, and all sorts of rusted machines. Empty tin cans were strewn everywhere. None of us wanted to sit down. Through the translator, he told us that he was a World War II veteran with many service metals. His mother had been a famous singer in Ukraine many years before, but now he lived worse than a pauper.

As we shared with him about the work of Ebenezer and the need for him to return to Israel, he listened but didn't seem interested. I felt like he was going to tell us to leave, but he didn't, continuing to listen as Roman shared Scripture through the translator. He went on to tell us that he had suffered a heart attack and had had some operations. We stressed that if he returned to Israel, he could get much better medical care than was available in Ukraine. He seemed to ignore that. He said that he wanted to stay in Ukraine to build a monument to his dead mother. Again, here was this stronghold, this "tie to the dead." But then he told us that he had some relatives living in Europe, and when he completed this monument, he may consider Israel.

Based on his countenance, this was an unexpected, amazing breakthrough. Again, we witnessed the power of God's Word at work, and we believed the Lord for this man. These were His people. He only called us to take them home. The hearts that listened were the ones He would bring home: "The remnant will return, the remnant of Jacob" (Isaiah 10:21).

Our next visit proved to be my first real difficult situation. When the old woman invited us into her apartment, I immediately became nauseous. The smells were overwhelming—a noxious combination of dried sweat, foul breath, urine, and waste. I sidled up to another volunteer who was wearing a winter coat with a hood and stuck my face inside it to avoid breathing the air. I tried to motion to the translator to make this visit quick. She and Roman began sharing the good news of Aliyah and the Scriptures with the woman. She shared that her forty-seven-year-old son, who was very sick, lived with her, and she adamantly said she had no desire to go to Israel. We asked her what would happen to her son when she died, and she said that someone would take care of him. Somehow, she had confidence that things would work out. I thought again of the remnant, as prophesied through Isaiah: "For though your people, O Israel, be as the sand of the sea, a remnant of them will return" (Isaiah 10:22).

We gave her a larger than normal food parcel. She immediately looked into it to see what we had brought, thanking us over and over.

As the team was getting ready to leave, I went outside to get some fresh air. I couldn't stay in there one minute longer. As I took in one deep breath after another, I began to feel better. I had never experienced such foulness. I was later told that this wasn't unusual with some of the older people in the flats. It was hard for them to go outside when the lifts didn't work, they had a hard time climbing the stairs, and a sick person didn't get much fresh air unless someone helped him or her outside. This woman could barely get around herself.

Sometimes it was hard to catch our breath—literally, for me—after leaving a flat like that one. The hopelessness and darkened souls were so apparent that our only choice was to believe that the Lord would do a miracle in the midst of it. As we spoke His Word to the hearts of His people, God was speaking to our hearts over and over again about the remnant and about being there to call forth His people. He would do the rest: "But I will gather the remnant of My flock out of all countries where I have driven them, and bring them back to their folds" (Jeremiah 23:3). The Word of the Lord was taking such a firm grip on our hearts that on a few occasions the Scriptures just flowed from our lips as the translator read them in Russian.

We were greeted at the next flat by a lovely old lady. I'd decided to excuse myself and wait for the team outside if this apartment was as bad as the one we had just left. Thankfully it wasn't, although that smell seemed to stay with me. I felt like it had permeated my clothes. I worried about not being able to wash them and about getting nauseous again. In the midst of this kind of thing, we knew that we had to pray for ourselves, and the Lord would have to help us know what to do.

As we visited with this old lady, we did our normal introductions and shared about Aliyah. She wasn't at all open to leaving, telling us that her family and children were all in Ukraine. She said her family was okay, her life was established, and she saw no need to leave. We, of course, didn't force anything on her. We prayed for her and her family and thanked her for letting us come and share with her. As we left, the scripture that came to Roman's heart was Jeremiah 16:16: "Behold, I will send for many fishermen…and they shall fish them. Afterward I will send for many hunters, and they will hunt them from every mountain and every hill and out of the holes of the rocks."

We decided to see one more family before heading home for lunch. The house was in the countryside, surrounded by a tall, green gate. As we banged on the gate, I thought about the days of the communist regime, wondering if these houses were walled-in to have some measure of privacy. The weather had turned cold during our time in Kirovograd, and we felt it through our clothes as we waited for a response. Finally, an old babushka opened the gate and greeted us. As we stepped inside, we saw a house that was falling apart. It was made of cement, which was broken in many places. Dogs were running loose everywhere in the yard, and I wondered if they all belonged to her.

Inside the house, the conditions were deplorable, not even fit for the dogs. The wooden floors were creaky and broken, covered with dirt and sand. This house had a smell, but not as intense as the earlier one.

The woman introduced us to her sixty-two-year-old son, Vasily, who lived with her. He was busy in the corner, using a hotplate to heat the room. He had an open hole in his neck from some type of operation, and it looked as if it shouldn't be exposed to the air and the obvious unsanitary conditions of this house. He had much difficulty speaking. It was hard for me to look at him, and I found myself turning away. Like so many people we'd visited, he was in dire need of medical care.

The team shared about how the God of Israel was calling His people home. Vasily just stared at us, his heart obviously hearing this for the first time. He was a sweet and simple man, and he was open to all we were saying. He said he'd be willing to go to Israel, but that his mother wouldn't budge. He said he'd try and persuade her. But the elderly had seen and experienced so much devastation and poverty of life and spirit, why should they believe that things could be better for them now? God and God alone would be able to convince her. We had to keep reminding ourselves of this and of the miracles we'd already experienced in some of the families we'd visited.

Though God was calling these people home through us, the church, many of them clung to the old ways of life. Their years under communism had darkened their minds to their God and to what their faith is all about. My heart went out to them as I thanked God for my own faith. All I knew was that the Lord was faithful. So we continued to believe Him for this family. We left them with a food parcel and some brochures and made our way back to our flat for a desperately-needed meal.

There it was once again, out of nothing, like the way Jesus fed the multitudes with five loaves and two fish (Matthew 14:17). We emptied our hearts and minds for the day and settled in for the night. The next day was Shabbat and we had been asked to share at a messianic fellowship.

Day Six of Fishing

The service started at ten. We were dressed and ready to leave by nine, so we arrived on time. For a change, the building the fellowship had rented was a pleasant one, old but lovely, and well cared for. The believers were few, but very warm and kind to us.

About half way through the service, the rabbi asked our translator to share and introduce her guests. She did, and then she shared about the ministry and all that the Lord was doing concerning Aliyah. Roman then shared the Scriptures. The rabbi reinforced what Roman had read, repeating some of the verses from Jeremiah. After a week of visiting all the run-down apartments and being in the midst of so much poverty and darkness, it was refreshing and life-affirming to be among believers in a church setting. The language barrier didn't matter at all. We broke bread with them and shared wine at the Lord's Table.

Because it was Shabbat and we wanted and needed to have our rest, we decided to visit only one family that afternoon. Also, it was getting darker earlier now, and the weather was colder. So, filled with the joy and laughter of the service, we made our way in the van to the flat.

The family we visited was another old couple. As we shared the ministry with them and read the Scriptures, we could see that the woman was very open. She told us through the translator that her husband had had a stroke and was paralyzed on one side of his body. She was concerned because he couldn't sit in a wheelchair. Through God's Word we assured her that we could get him to Israel because it was God's plan for them. "I will seek what was lost and bring back what was driven away, bind up the broken and strengthen what was sick" (Ezekiel 34:16).

Then the lady told us that she was a Holocaust survivor and shared an experience. When she was about eleven, a Ukrainian family hid her and her mother from the Nazis. Her mother was hidden between layers of blankets and pillows on a bed when the Nazi soldiers searched the Ukrainian woman's home. She held the little girl's hand as she told the troops, "Can't you see this is a Ukrainian girl? There are no Jews here." And the soldiers left. But the woman told us that she eventually wound up in a concentration camp in Romania. She didn't give us any other details but said that she was interviewed for one of Stephen Spielberg's documentaries.

She had made tea and cookies for us. Before serving them, she put a tablecloth down. We were told that when this is done in a Jewish home, it means that the guests are welcome to stay as long as they want. This was such a refreshing visit for the whole team. The entire day, in fact, was just what we all needed—the messianic fellowship in the morning, and then this gracious lady, after all she had been through, open to Aliyah. As we made our way back home, we thanked the Lord for continuing to watch over, care for, and direct us during our time here.

Seventh Day of Fishing

It was Sunday, and we had planned to go to the local charismatic church, which was about a five-minute walk from the flat. The other two volunteers met us, and we left as a group for the noon service.

The church had been started by Nigerian missionaries about six years before. The building was an old factory that looked like it dated back to the middle ages. Like many other factories throughout Ukraine, it had been closed down for a while and needed much work. But it was the Lord's house, and we were glad to be there.

The building filled up quickly, almost to overflowing. I couldn't help but think of all the beautiful churches back home that were so empty on Sundays. But these people were grateful just to have a place to come and worship where they could be protected from the elements. We took our seats and began to enjoy the music that started to play. Then a lady approached us, spoke with our translator, and invited us to sit up in the front row. She knew we were foreigners, and we were humbled by her graciousness.

Though the songs were in Russian, we recognized many that we sang in our own churches back home. It was wonderful to hear them sung in another language. We felt privileged to be there, in what once was a very dark place, witnessing the light of the Lord shining so brightly.

As I sat in the service, allowing the familiar music to wash over me, a slideshow of the past two months clicked through my mind: Leaving our children. Arriving in Ukraine. The bathrooms. The base. The train stations and the hopeful Olim. Our waterless flat with its close quarters. The lovely babushka. The families and the apartments we'd visited. The Scriptures transforming lives right in front of our eyes. Only God could do something on a scale like this.

As the pastor neared the end of his sermon, there was an altar call. Five people went forward to receive the Lord. I hadn't seen this kind of acceptance of salvation in a long time. Then there was a healing line, and the pastor prayed for all those who came forward.

By the time we left, it was midday and raining—one of those Sundays you just want to curl up with a good book and a cup of hot chocolate. Our translator told us that it was not uncommon for the seasons to change from one day to the next, from autumn to winter overnight.

It was good and necessary for us to have a day of rest from the physical and emotional energy it took to visit families. I thought of how, after he slew all the prophets of Baal, Elijah pleaded, "It is enough!" (1 Kings 19:4). And then how, after he rested, he "...ate and drank; and he went in the strength of that food forty days and forty nights as far as Horeb, the mountain of God" (1 Kings 19:8). So that day we returned to the flat for a restorative dinner and some fellowship.

We'd been here over a week now and really had our bathroom routine well rehearsed. We were still seven people and a baby in a tiny flat with no running water all day long and no electricity for most of the day. Yet the Lord stayed over the whole situation. The only thing that began to wear on me was the effort required to communicate. The constant translation, the need to continually listen, speak, and listen again, would cause light headaches from time to time. But when I thought about how doubly hard and tiring this was on our translator, I was able to set it aside.

When it was my turn in the bathroom, I looked in the mirror and was thankful I'd gotten a perm before I left the States. For not having washed my hair in a week, it didn't look that bad. I tried to read some Scripture that night, but surprisingly, I was too tired. Our day of rest only showed me that I needed more. I curled up next to Roman, thanking the Lord in advance for what He was going to do through us on Monday.

Eighth and Last Day of Fishing

This was our last day of fishing, and a busy one.

Our first visit was to a woman who, surprisingly, spoke English. She was a retired school teacher, widowed, in her sixties. She shared that she had children and grandchildren who wanted to go to Israel and that they observed the Jewish holidays.

After going over the specifics of the ministry, Roman and I shared the Scriptures with her. As we did, our voices began to break, and we had to pause. We were overcome by what the Lord was doing through us—sharing His Word, without a translator, using our own voices and our own hearts. I looked right into this woman's face and spoke tenderly to her, remembering God's instruction, "Speak comfort to Jerusalem" (Isaiah 40:2).

The fact that the Lord would choose the likes of us to do something like this, far beyond our natural capacity, continued to astound us. Without any Bible-school background, we were turning the light on for people who had been in religious oppression for nearly seventy years. This was on a scale that was never really explained to us. But it once again proved the words of Jesus: "With men this is impossible, but with God all things are possible" (Matthew 19:26).

Our next flat was not too far away. The family consisted of a mother, who was partially blind, and a daughter, who was in a tech school. The mother wanted her daughter to finish school before making any plans for Israel. She told us that they had made plans before to make Aliyah, but they'd had to cancel the trip because of illness. Since then, she had heard conflicting reports about life in Israel from friends and was now hesitant to leave.

We reassured her with the statistics we had about all those who had already fled this nation—nearly a million people over the previous eight years. This seemed to encourage her. We left her with a food parcel and could only believe, as we had in so many other situations, that the Lord would work on her heart.

At our next flat, we were greeted by a couple in their eighties. I came to realize that the elderly were those who God had dispersed to the four corners of the earth, the ones prophesied about in Deuteronomy. "Then the Lord will scatter you among all peoples, from one end of the earth to the other" (Deuteronomy 28:64). And they were the ones He was faithfully calling back: "And I will bring them out from the peoples and gather them from the countries, and will bring them to their own land" (Ezekiel 34:13).

As they invited us in, I caught my breath. The smell of poverty and sickness once again overcame me. The conditions were horrifying. The kitchen was ancient and everything in it looked broken. I wondered if the old stove in the corner even worked. There were no conveniences of any kind. A small, rusted pail of sprouting potatoes stood in a corner. The fact that old and retired people were forced to live like this spoke of the country's lack of care louder than anything else.

Settling on some chairs that I was afraid would break at any moment, we shared the work of Ebenezer, and then Roman shared the Scriptures. Through the translator, the couple told us that they had two sisters living in Israel. When we talked of all the modern conveniences, the apartments with running water and electric, and the medical care available there, they brightened and said "yes" to Israel.

I was awed at how the Lord moved on the hearts of the older generation. How hard it must be for a person to make a change of this magnitude at the end of his or her life. Who did I know in their eighties who would leave their country and start life over again? This was nothing less than a miraculous fulfillment of prophecy. "I will give you a new heart and put a new spirit within you" (Ezekiel 36:26). It was not over for them. They would still see and partake of the land before leaving this earth. They had paid a high price to do so. But I believe God allowed

Kitchen in one of the flats

them, like Sarah, to live into old age before birthing their miracle, so that He would get the glory.

Just as the Lord had called Abraham, he was now calling the elderly to return. How amazing and astounding this was. With my own eyes I was seeing Scripture come alive. "Then you shall dwell in the land that I gave to your fathers; you shall be My people, and I will be your God" (Ezekiel 36:28). The more I saw prophecy being fulfilled, the more I knew that I will never fully understand what we as believers are caught up in. The Lord Himself, says so: "For as the heavens are higher than the earth, so are My ways higher than your ways, and My thoughts higher than your thoughts" (Isaiah 55:9).

We left that flat and headed for the next family, about twenty-five miles outside the city. As we drove, we couldn't stop talking about this couple. We realized that with the time it would take them to get all their documents, they could very well be on the last sailing of this year with us. Being able to escort to Israel someone we fished for, especially people as elderly as these, would be, in a sense, like giving birth—prophetic birth to the fulfillment of God's Word.

By the time we reached the next family it was late afternoon. The sun had gone down, and it was getting cold and dark. At this hour, most people are off the streets, and there's little, if any, lighting. It wasn't safe to walk in the dark in Ukraine, as the roads were full of potholes, garbage, and debris. You could get seriously hurt tripping and falling over old pieces of metal, broken glass, or cement. Some roads were partially torn up, as if a gas line were being replaced, or some other major work was being done. But the road would just be left like that. Finding our families in the dark was difficult, which is why we tried to make all of our visits before sunset. But at times like these, when we had to deal with less than desirable conditions, we knew the Lord would protect and direct us. And He did.

We finally found our family and made our way to the door. We were met by a woman who was involved with the Jewish community in the area and who knew where many of them lived. She invited us in to the obviously poverty-stricken flat and introduced us to a brother and sister who lived there. He was a World War II veteran, the years of hardship and the poverty of soul and spirit etched on his sagging face. His sister was a retired history teacher and had recently suffered a stroke.

Through the translator, we introduced ourselves and explained the work of Ebenezer and Aliyah. They listened, but they didn't seem interested in going to Israel. And then, with a bit of an edge, they told us so. We didn't push anything on them, but just continued to talk about other things until the atmosphere eased. Then we took our cue, prayed for them, left a food parcel, and headed for the van.

It was getting late, and we still needed to see one more family before returning home for the night. The woman who had met us at the door joined us in the van to direct us to our final family, who lived nearby.

Through the translator, the next couple began to share that they had two sons. One was living in Siberia and was in the Russian army. The other lived in Israel. The wife said that she did not want to go there. She said she felt she could be more help to her sons if she stayed in Ukraine and that she had many relatives here and couldn't leave them. This wasn't uncommon, people not wanting to leave loved ones. And it made me think of how difficult it was to leave my own children, which elicited an ache that threatened to overpower me. Inwardly I turned to the Lord, who faithfully gave me the grace to continue to minister to these people.

We tried to encourage this couple through the Scriptures, showing them that now was the time to go home to Israel, that the doors wouldn't be open forever, and that the Lord had sent us, His "fishermen," to "fish them" (Jeremiah 16:16). Then we prayed with them, gave them a food parcel and brochures, and left for "home."

On the drive, I thought about how some of God's people were receptive about returning to their homeland, while others were closed to it. After having lived under such oppression of spirit for so long, I couldn't understand how they still seemed to hold some measure of loyalty to this country. But if oppression is all you know, I suppose it's all you have. So many Jewish people were rooted in this land and wanted to be buried with their families, their sense of duty toward the dead seemingly stronger than toward the living.

We arrived back at the flat ready to crash. As usual, the babushka had a wonderful dinner, our last, ready and waiting. How grateful I was, we all were, to this woman. And I knew that she was grateful as well, as the Lord had blessed her with a bit of extra income for housing and feeding us.

It had been a long day, and we were all exhausted. After supper it was time for the nightly chores, bathroom duties, and getting ourselves together for the trip back to the base. The fact that I had not had a shower in nearly two weeks was a testimony to my own heart that "I can do all things through Christ who strengthens me" (Phil. 4:13). I could not believe it had been that long since I had washed my hair. There was no guarantee that there would be hot water on the base, so I knew I needed to do it that night. Though the situation had nothing to do with having poor personal hygiene, I was embarrassed at the thought of telling anyone back home that I hadn't showered or washed my hair in almost two weeks. But by the time our work in Ukraine was over, the word "embarrassment" wouldn't even be part of our vocabulary.

I got my dishpan of warm water from the stove and headed to the bathroom. I tried to make believe that I was a child in the bathtub. Kids don't have a problem using the same water to bathe and wash their hair, so why did I? This experience, as unimportant as it sounds, actually stripped away some of my inhibitions, leaving me more willing to touch the culture and not be afraid of it all the time. I can't really explain it, but it was the simple things that broke us, that seemed to slam our hearts like a hammer.

Final Day in Kirovograd

It was now the morning of our last day. By the time we took our turns in the bathroom, had breakfast, met up with the other two team members, prayed, and loaded all our luggage and belongings onto the van, it was almost noon. As we were saying our goodbyes to the babushka, her daughters, and the baby, the phone rang. It was Sophia, telling us that the last family we visited yesterday had decided to make Aliyah. What a parting gift! We all shouted, "Hallelujah!" It was just incredible how these things happened. The Lord had moved upon their hearts during the night. It was such an encouragement, such a repeated confirmation of Isaiah 55:11: "So is my word that goes forth from my mouth; It will not return to me void, but it shall accomplish what I please, and it shall prosper in thing for which I sent it."

With hugs, smiles, and tears, we left this wonderful family who had become just that to us. Before leaving, I slipped some American money into the pocket of the babushka's apron. Roman and I wished we could have done more. But our budget was already tight, and we knew we just had to trust the Lord for her, as well as for ourselves.

It was decided that Roman would drive back to Odessa. I felt so much safer with Roman at the wheel than I did on our way to Kirovograd. Our driver was young and had been a bit reckless at times.

During the five-hour drive, I remembered not to drink too much. But we did stop once at a fuel station that had a bathroom. Roman used it, warning us that it was unsanitary—a concrete structure with just a hole—and that there were no lights anywhere. We were thankful for the tiny flashlights we brought with us. It was these hurdles, the lack of basic necessities we took for granted back home, that pressed us. But the more we were pressed, the more we overcame, reminding me of Paul's words in 2 Corinthians 4:8–9: "We are hard pressed on every side, yet not crushed; we are perplexed, but not in despair; persecuted, but not forsaken; struck down, but not destroyed."

We arrived at the base just before dinner. The measure of civilization provided on the base, as meager as it was, made our return surreal, as if we'd been in the catacombs for the past ten days. We were greeted warmly by all the other volunteers and told that Roman and I could keep our same room. This was wonderful to hear, as usually when you return from a fishing trip, you are assigned different rooms.

We had dinner and then gathered in the prayer room for the daily praise and worship meeting. The spiritual leader shared a short message and thanked the Lord for our safe return.

After the meeting, we brought our luggage up to our room. Instead of seeing its deficiencies, we were so grateful for the privacy it offered, including its tiny bathroom. To be able to spend time by ourselves, without five other people constantly around, was a treat. It made me realize that you don't appreciate being alone until you're never alone. And finally removed from that small apartment with five women, I could see the liberation on Roman's face. How hard this must have been for him. But the whole time we were there, Roman was obedient, putting the situation behind him and going forward with what he had to do. I was so proud of him, and I told him so.

Though the last ten days had rendered us worn and wrung out, I was yet to experience the full effect of the work we'd just done. But I knew we'd have a day or two of rest on the base, and I was eagerly anticipating that. Then we were to begin the trips to the train stations again, picking up more Olim for the next sailing, scheduled in about a week. This was the ship we would be on.

While in Kirovograd, there hadn't been much occasion to think about the kids. Other than the few conversations we'd had among the team about our families, we had been one hundred percent engaged with the Jewish families. If we weren't visiting with and ministering to them, we were processing our time with them, either internally or as a team. But now that the work was behind us, I took a big, spiritual sigh. And with that release came the ache for my children.

When we got into bed, I sidled up to my husband. As I wrapped my arms under and around his broad back, he clasped my hands to his chest. In the beats of his stalwart heart I could feel the kindred longing for home, for the kids, for the life we left behind. And just when my own ache became almost unbearable, the Lord whispered a gentle but firm reminder: *"I will take care of your children, as you take care of mine."* And beneath His blanket of grace, I fell into a deep sleep.

Chapter 9 ❧

Bringing His People Home

Behold, I will lift My hand in an oath to the nations…They shall bring your sons in their arms, and your daughters shall be carried on their shoulders.

—Isaiah 49:22

AS MORNING LIGHT nudged me awake, I listened for the babushka bustling about in the kitchen and the baby's playful banter. It wasn't until I opened my eyes that I remembered we were back on the base. Our time in Kirovograd in that tiny apartment had knit us to that family. As glad as I was to have our privacy back, I missed them.

Our health had been stellar while we were away. I had felt fine, just tired, the night before. But as I got up, those ten days bore down. My lower back ached badly, and my head began to throb. My stomach churned as I headed for the bathroom, where I wound up spending most of the day. Although Roman didn't feel as bad as I did, his pallor and stoop spoke of his exhaustion.

As I said before, we'd been warned about how many volunteers return from fishing trips physically sick and emotionally spent. And how could it be avoided? Besides the endless climbing of stairs and the close living that poverty demands, the sickness and unsanitary conditions in the flats we visited practically guaranteed ill health. But thankfully, the Lord kept us strong while we needed to be, and now we could crash.

I couldn't eat much at breakfast. Afterwards, the leaders laid hands on me, anointed me with oil, and prayed for me. This was normal procedure for volunteers who were sick after returning from the field. Two of the base leaders were Americans, and it was comforting, especially with feeling as bad as I was, to be prayed for in my own language.

The day after returning from a fishing trip was always a day of rest, and I continued to do so that day. I meditated on Psalm 23, especially on verse 2: "He makes me lie down in green pastures, he leads me beside still waters, He restores my soul." Between visits to the bathroom, I took advantage of that first day to try and get some emails out to the kids. Unlike the short messages we'd send each other at home, these turned into books. There was just so much to say, so much to report. It had now been nearly two weeks since we had received or sent any emails, and I was hungry to talk to my kids. Because we had to share the computer with the other volunteers, I tried not to be too long. But I probably was, as I was losing track of time in the excitement of writing.

Just as I was finishing up a description of our fishing trip, the lights on the base went out—and so did the computer, a black screen swallowing up my nearly half-hour email. I tried not to cry, but couldn't hold back the tears. These were the kinds of things we had to learn to slough off. It wasn't easy, but in time, we did. I couldn't see it then, but the Lord was using these frustrations to build up the level of patience we'd need to go forward.

A group of volunteers that had just returned from a sailing to Haifa had brought a newspaper back. At home, the news was at our fingertips. But here, we were isolated and starved for information. The trip back to Odessa on the ship took several days, so the news was a week old. But to us it was like it happened yesterday. There was usually only a single paper that got passed around. By the time we got it, it was worn, torn, and smudged. But we devoured it.

After that first day, I felt much better. And it was a good thing too, because by the second day our schedule was in full swing. The ship we were sailing on was departing in a week, and we were back to picking up the Olim at the train station, five or more families a day. We'd get up at three in the morning and have a quick breakfast and a short prayer meeting. We'd always pray that the trains would arrive on time and that we'd have no trouble finding our families. And this, thank God, usually turned out to be the case.

Roman drove the Lorry, while two other mini-buses ran shuttle services between two Ebenezer bases and the train stations. In all, we were picking up about sixty-five Olim per day. There were adults, grandparents, small children, infants, and many invalids. The disabled were the most difficult to transport. None arrived with wheelchairs, but Ebenezer provided them. As the older people hobbled or had to be assisted off the trains, we'd put them in the wheelchairs and push them to the Lorry. There were no ramps or handicap provisions whatsoever, so this took extra effort. In this country, travel for the handicapped was out of the question, unless they had a family traveling with them.

As usual, the luggage was a constant drain. Each bag had to be taken from the trains and loaded onto the Lorry. This was part of my job, and the walk from the station to where the Lorry was parked seemed like miles. After a few of these trips, my hands hurt terribly, and my palms blistered. But one day, in the midst of it, a ten-year-old girl came off the train with a bouquet of small, red carnations and handed them to me in a gesture of thanks. Moments like these made the blisters disappear and the Lord reappear.

Once the bags were loaded onto the Lorry, we'd drive to the bases, where the bags had to be off-loaded, carried into the corpuses on the bases, and then moved to the rooms. Then on sailing day the whole procedure started again, with each of us handling those bags a minimum of five times before they got to the ship.

As I mentioned before, neither I nor Roman, with all of his years as a marine, had ever experienced or endured this type of (literally) back-breaking work. Roman had worked as a mover for over twelve years, so this was somewhat familiar to him. It never ceased to amaze me how the Lord used every talent and experience we had. Though he occasionally complained that his back hurt, Roman never let it bother him. Many of the volunteers were young, in their twenties, and not used to this kind of manual labor. I was proud of my husband, a good thirty years older than most of the volunteers, lifting and hoisting without a complaint.

But I worried about Roman, especially with the diet we'd been on. He is a man who loves food and eats heartily. And this effort demanded nutritious food—large portions of red meat, meals rich in iron and protein, not the meager amounts we were getting on the base. It was obvious that the Lord had to continue to remain "… the strength of my heart and my portion forever" (Psalm 73:26). So much of our fortitude was drawn from Scripture, proving that "…the word of God is living and powerful" (Hebrews 4:12).

As usual, the day before sailing was electric, especially for Roman and me. We had been anticipating our one trip to Haifa ever since we arrived, especially after hearing about the food and relaxation from the other volunteers who had sailed.

As part of the pre-sailing-day activity, we prepared about seventy-five sandwiches. On sailing day, all of us would be up at the crack of dawn, and by noon, the Olim would finally be going through customs and boarding the ship. By this time, after having dealt with the luggage, the volunteers would be exhausted, famished, and depleted, so we made sure to bring along some sustenance. The making of these sandwiches was a production unto itself, taking almost two hours. There were twelve loaves of bread, a three-pound block of cheese, three rolls of mystery meat (something like bologna, but not as tasty), and jars of mayonnaise. There were six of us, three on either side of a banquet-length table, and we began the process of slicing and assembling.

After we were finished and had wrapped all the sandwiches, our translator came into the room. She took a piece of meat that was lying on the table, tasted it, made a face, then went into the kitchen and returned with one of the babushkas. She also tasted a piece of the meat and made a face. There was no translation needed. The meat we had just used to make seventy-five sandwiches was bad. With the electrical blackouts, refrigeration had probably been an issue. Every sandwich had to be unwrapped, the meat removed, and more cheese added. But the translator told us not to throw the meat away, that the babushkas wanted to take it home. I assumed they wanted it for their dogs, but she told us that they knew how to fry or boil it so as not to get sick. I thought about what we throw away at home, about the restaurants and all the food that goes to waste. It made me ashamed.

Sailing Day

We are going to be part of the actual voyage of the Lord's people to Israel! This thought overshadowed every other as we did our part in the horrendous loading, unloading, and waiting at the Odessa port. Throughout the morning, as we took our stations among the Olim, we tried speaking with them as best we could. It was almost impossible without a translator, but we could understand some of what the children said. When one little boy asked if we were going on the ship with them, our excitement made us feel like children ourselves. With huge smiles, we told him that we were, replying in Russian, "Da!"

As the loading of the ship came to an end, the volunteers who were sailing boarded. We were tired, hungry, and sore, but we made our way to the front of the ship to wave our goodbyes. It took all the energy left in us just to climb the stairs to the top deck. The week of handling all that luggage and then repeating it this morning without escalators or conveyor belts had frayed every fiber. We wanted a bed more than anything.

We stood with all the Olim on the upper deck of the ship, which was docked directly across from the top level of the port building. This was where all the families stood to wave goodbye to the Olim who were sailing. Families spoke loudly back and forth, many with video cameras held to their faces. At last, the voice of the ship's captain came over the loudspeaker with a final boarding announcement. Within minutes, the gangplank was hoisted, the ropes at the dock were untied, and a grinding sound signaled the mechanical lifting of the anchor. We could see the volunteers that were left behind, as we had been the last time, at the portside far below us. They held a big Israeli flag, waved, and sang Hebrew songs. As the ship moved slowly from the port in a cloud of gray smoke, we waved back.

Within fifteen minutes, we were on the open sea. We were still on the top deck. Looking down into the water I understood why it is called the Black Sea. There wasn't a trace of blue, blue-green, or aqua. Just as it had on the fishing trip days before, a sense of spiritual oppression came over me. There was such darkness over this nation. But, I reminded myself, we were sailing through it. We were headed toward the light.

We were returning God's people to the land of Israel, where it is sunny and bright, where "...they shall obtain joy and gladness, and sorrow and sighing shall flee away" (Isaiah 35:10). As quickly as the dark thoughts came, they left. And I realized that I was very, very cold. The weather had shifted dramatically, and we all headed down to our cabins.

Ours was a small cabin on the lower deck. It was simple, with two bunk beds and a tiny bathroom. But it had a shower, sink, and toilet. To us, the accommodations were five-star. The most precious amenities were the hot water any time we wanted it and the electricity that worked day and night. I began to understand what the volunteers who had sailed before kept telling us: "Everything will come back to you—all the comforts of home. You can take a shower every day, even twice a day if you want. You will feel like a human being again." The thought of washing my hair in the shower was more exciting than if I'd won the lottery.

As I unpacked, I thought about what we'd done so far in Ukraine. We'd picked up hundreds of Olim from the train station, handled thousands of pounds of luggage, prepared for two sailings, and fished for about thirty families. And now, here we were on a ship to Israel. We went from one environment to another, one country to another, each situation requiring a chameleon's skin. We believed in this work with all of our hearts, which made each transition palatable, no matter how hard or draining. Every now and then, I saw Roman's military training kick in. His steadfast spirit, his determination to see our work through, was my inspiration. I was so glad and thankful to be with him. He and the Lord were my sources of strength.

Roman was preparing for a shower. When he took off his t-shirt, I cringed. The welts on his back were fresh and raw, and I had to look away. Many of the suitcases had been secured with ropes and belts. The repeated hoisting of bags had rubbed these haphazard ties right through the men's jackets, scarring their backs. I couldn't stand to see how bruised Roman was. But I had to keep believing that he would heal over the next few days on the ship, that the good food and rest would restore him.

As Roman took his shower, steam rolled beneath the door. It looked like that fake smoke they use at rock concerts. Having not had a shower the whole time we were in Kirovograd and then only a lukewarm one on the base before we left, I can't tell you how giddy this made me. When it was my turn in the bathroom, I felt like the Queen of Sheba. After we'd showered and rested, we barely recognized ourselves, especially the spring in our step as we made our way to the dining room.

Another thing the volunteers who had sailed before us raved about was the food. "You won't believe it. It's absolutely delicious, nothing like base food. You'll think you are on a luxury liner. You can even have seconds." And they were right!

The dining room was huge, with beautifully set tables and colorful tablecloths. There was real silver, real glassware, and real dinner plates, not the saucer-sized ones we had gotten used to. Coffee cups with saucers were at every seat, as were napkins. These were luxuries we didn't have at the base, and it took me a few minutes to take it all in. And as I did, I was overcome with God's mercy and love, how His heart was so much in this work. He had found His people; He was gathering them home, calling the nations to help them in every way. He was setting a table for them, preparing a banquet for them, rejoicing over them. "For they shall feed their flocks and lie down, and no one shall make them afraid... The Lord your God in your midst...will rejoice over you with singing" (Zephaniah 3:13, 17).

The dining room seated about 150, so there were two seatings for dinner. We were on the first shift, with the families who had children. The volunteers sat together at a separate table, which was next to the huge windows. This would be our assigned table throughout the trip. We could eat our meals and watch waves crash against the ship. It was breathtaking, and at this early point, hard to believe. The trying situations we'd been through so far, the frustrations, anxieties, and fear we'd experienced seemed nothing to us now. I thought that this is what it must be like when we are really with the Lord. We won't remember all that we went through. We won't remember all the tough times, the pressure, and the heaviness. It will be glorious.

The waitress came and offered us a choice for dinner. This stunned me. I had forgotten what it was like to go out to eat and have the luxury of selecting what I wanted.

Dinner table for volunteers on the ship

We could choose chicken or beef. I chose chicken with rice, while Roman chose steak and potatoes. I was relieved and thankful for the iron and protein he'd be getting.

As the other volunteers made their choices, I watched the Olim file in and take their places at the tables. Necks craned and eyes widened at the abundance around them. I was sure they were experiencing a joy similar to mine as the music of children's laughter and conversations in Russian, English, German, and Afrikaans filled the room.

Within minutes, the waitress brought our meals, along with a huge salad for the whole table to share. The salad was incredibly fresh and beautiful, with tomatoes, carrots, and multi-colored lettuces. I hadn't had a salad since we arrived in Ukraine, and I felt as if I could eat the whole thing myself. The food looked delicious, and the portions were huge. I knew I wouldn't be able to finish mine—I think my stomach had shrunk. But Roman was in his glory. He had waited and worked hard to have this opportunity to literally eat his heart out.

The food was delicious. I was again experiencing, the way I did with privacy after our fishing trip, that you don't realize how much you enjoy something until it's taken away. We hadn't had good, substantial food like this since leaving home. As I looked around the room, I could see the Olim going through a similar realization. Only with them, I suspected that they'd never had food like this. When dinner was almost over, I saw many of them wrapping up their leftovers in napkins to bring back to their cabins.

After dinner we took a walk on the deck. We met a Ukrainian pastor who spoke English very well. Ebenezer holds spots on the sailings for pastors in Ukraine who support the work of Aliyah. The ministry wants to get as many churches and pastors alongside this work as possible. When the pastor told us that he knew Jonathan Bernis, the founder of Jewish Voice Ministries, we told him that Jonathan had prayed over us at a conference in 1997. He had laid his hands on our stomachs and said, "May this burden for Israel stick to your spirits like glue."

Before we turned in for the night, Roman and I walked to the bow of the ship. It was cold and windy, but incredible to stand there and watch the tip of the ship slice through the water. With the breeze in our faces and our jackets ruffling, I felt like we were on the Titanic. When Roman told me to look up at the sky, I almost choked on the wind rushing into my gaping mouth. The only thing I could compare this to was when I had gone to the Planetarium in New York City. Only this was real. On the open sea, against complete darkness, the stars lit up the night sky like thousands of tiny, neon lights. The clarity was so sharp that we could point out all the constellations. There were even shooting stars. The Lord was blessing us with His creation, His extravagance, and His brilliance. "The heavens declare the glory of God; and the firmament shows His handiwork" (Psalm 19:1). It made us think of what God said to Abraham, "Look now toward heaven, and count the stars if you are able to number them...So shall your descendents be" (Genesis 15:5). And here we were, bringing those very descendents home.

It eventually got too cold, so we made our way back to our cabin. It had been a big day, and our beds had been in the back of our minds since we boarded. We tucked ourselves into our bunks, feeling the motion of the ship on the water. In our eight-day roundtrip between Odessa and Haifa, we would cover 2,500 miles of open sea. I'd never been on a ship before and didn't know whether or not I'd get seasick. But before I knew it, the gentle sway rocked me to sleep—as if I were in the very arms of the Lord.

Second Day of Sailing

We woke at 7:30 to an announcement over the loudspeaker that breakfast would be served at 8:00. We washed and dressed quickly, then made our way to the dining room. Again, the tables were beautifully set, and the food was delicious and plentiful.

After breakfast, the volunteers met in the lounge for morning praise and worship. This would be standard for each day on the ship, and whoever could play an instrument usually led the worship. After this, we were given the schedule for the next three days and were told what our responsibilities would be. There was a children's' program in the afternoons that we would all need to be involved in, because of the number of kids on the ship. We were also told that before arriving in Haifa, we would have a farewell meeting with all of the Olim.

Bosphorous Straits

Olim on deck while passing through Bosphorous Straits

After the meeting, it was announced over the loudspeaker that we were arriving in the Bosphorous Straits, which divide Istanbul, Turkey, into the Asian and European sides. We had been told ahead of time how picturesque this was, so we took our cameras out to the bow of the ship.

The Straits are so narrow that it felt like you could reach out and touch the landscape. The day was bright and clear, the sun at our backs. The ship slowed as we sailed toward the ancient city—Istanbul is almost 800 years old. There were dozens of mosques scattered across the hills of the city, their towering minarets gleaming all the colors of the rainbow against the morning sun. I couldn't believe it, but we were hearing Muslim prayers.

How magnificent is my God in all the earth that we were Christians passing through a Muslim country with a shipload of Jews bound for Israel? "A highway shall be there…and it shall be called the Highway of Holiness… and the ransomed of the Lord shall return" (Isaiah 35:8, 10).

The Olim had flown onto the deck and seemed as excited as we were, shouting and pointing. Many of them had never before left the former Soviet Union. This was their liberation crossing, their maiden voyage into a brand-new world. They would be the pioneers for their families; they would begin the legacy in Israel for their seed. "I will make you an eternal excellence, a joy of many generations" (Isaiah 60:15).

We walked from one side of the ship to the other, trying to take everything in. The European side was spotted with large waterfront homes. There were castles and more minarets, the whole city of Istanbul exploding in brilliance and extravagance. And then, in what seemed like minutes but had been more like an hour, lunch was announced over the loudspeaker.

Being seated next to a window, feasting on delicious, nutritious food while gazing out on the water, made it feel like we were on a vacation cruise. The Bible says, "The Lord gave, and the Lord has taken away" (Job 1:21). This was, without a doubt, the giving part.

One of the things we were told to do in our morning meeting, in addition to helping with the children's program, was to interview at least two families. Ebenezer uses these often moving testimonies in their monthly brochures to help spread awareness about the prophetic move

Four generations making Aliyah

of Aliyah. We weren't told how to go about getting these interviews, so we just assumed we would ask the Olim for their permission to talk to them. They are very open and usually want to share, so after lunch we tried to find some familiar faces.

We located one family that we had helped in Odessa. They were a family of four, spanning four generations—a great-grandmother, grandmother, daughter, and grandson. Through the translator, they said they'd be happy to talk with us. We gathered in a corner of the lounge, where there were comfortable chairs and couches.

The great-grandmother was nearly ninety and could barely walk. From her chair, she shared how happy the whole family was to be making Aliyah. They were excited about the opportunities available in Israel. They were especially encouraged about the future of the grandson, as he was sure to get a good education.

Again, we were witnessing what we never thought possible—a ninety-year-old woman starting over. And again, we were witnessing prophetic fulfillment. "I will assemble the lame, I will gather the outcast and those whom I have afflicted; I will make the lame a remnant, and the outcast a strong nation" (Micah 4:6).

An hour later, in the same spot, we interviewed the next family, the largest we'd ever met. A fifty-nine-year-old woman, a doctor, was traveling with thirteen family members. Her parents and children were with her, as well as her nieces and nephews.

Through the translator, she echoed the difficulty of life in Ukraine and said that many professionals were out of work. She told us that twenty years before there had been a flood in her hometown, which resulted in sinkholes forming over a period of time. The holes were below the apartment buildings and affected the foundations to the point that some buildings collapsed. Many people died, their bodies never found. Public funds were not available for maintenance, and she said that people still live in these unsafe buildings because they have nowhere else to go.

The woman continued and shared what a massive move this was for them. But she said that when Ebenezer had presented this opportunity, there was no way she could turn it down. She told us that they were a very close family. I guess that's one positive thing I can say about

Building collapsed into a sinkhole in Odessa

Russia and Ukraine—people highly value their families and remain close throughout their lives.

From the interviews, we went to the children's program. Our Russian volunteer read the book of Moses, half on this day and half the next. Over the course of the next two days, we discussed all the adventures the Jewish people had during the first Exodus. We used this trip to Israel as a parallel, telling the children that this was their Exodus, that the Lord had called them out of the land of the north to return to Israel. Their little faces were attentive, wide-eyed, eagerly listening. Roman and I knew that this would be imprinted on their hearts forever.

The weather had been absolutely gorgeous, the water calm. All we needed when walking out on the deck was a windbreaker. I found that I had to make sure to continually get outside and take in the sea air. I began developing mild headaches and a stuffiness that made me tired. Our cabin was on the lower deck, where there was a slight smell of fuel, which could have been the cause. As we strolled along the walkways, we'd watch the faces of the Olim. Many were deep in thought, staring off into the horizon. We could only imagine what was going through their minds. I'm sure part of it was wondering what was ahead for them.

As Christians, we can take solace in knowing that our future rests in the Lord's hands. But for the Jewish people who don't know their Messiah, it must be very difficult. Still, Roman and I knew that God's plan for them was a good one (Jeremiah 29:11).

That night we had another wonderful dinner, followed by our fellowship meeting with the volunteers. After our worship time each night, one of us would share a small message, about fifteen minutes long, that was either a Scripture reading or a testimony combined with a Scripture reading. Every night, someone different spoke. For some this was hard, as many had never been put in a position of speaking before. But Ebenezer really encouraged this, as it was part of serving. It was preparation for speaking in the churches and at Jewish meetings and in the homes on fishing trips. To some, this aspect of the work seemed more burdensome than the physical side. But for Roman and me, it was basic. We had already lead morning prayer on the base, spoken at pre-sailing farewell meetings, and gotten our first fishing trip under our belt. The scope of involvement in Ebenezer's ministry was proving much wider than we had imagined.

Third Day of Sailing

Again, we woke to loudspeaker announcements. We heard "good morning" in English, plus the number of miles we had sailed, what the depth and temperature of the water was, and that breakfast would be served at 8:00. We had the choice of sleeping in if we were tired, but we would miss breakfast, so we never did. Some of the other volunteers, however, were more tired than hungry, so they opted for their beds.

After breakfast and our morning worship and prayer meeting, we took a walk on deck. It was another spectacular, balmy day. We were passing through the Aegean Sea and the Greek Islands. We actually saw Patmos, where John wrote the book of Revelation.

Our favorite spot was at the bow of the ship. As we leaned over on this bright blue morning, we were greeted by a school of dolphins. There were about five of them jumping in and out of the water, as if they were putting on a special show just for us. The children standing close by screamed in excitement. I knew this was like nothing they'd ever seen. I also knew that the Lord was gracing us with this spectacular happening.

In the children's meeting that day, we met one of the Olim who was not only a teacher but also a believer in Messiah. This was a confirmation to us that the Lord would use his own people as witnesses for Him once they were planted back in their land. "Then you shall dwell in the land that I gave to your fathers; you shall be My people, and I will be your God" (Ezekiel 36:28).

We were to arrive in Haifa the next day, so we had a planning meeting before bed. We were told that there would be a farewell meeting for the Olim and that once we got to the port we would have to offload luggage for anyone who was disabled. Hearing this, the lightheartedness I'd developed over these last two days gave way to dread. Israel was a modernized culture. I'd assumed there would be conveyor belts, escalators, or something to assist the process. But that was not the case. Even though there wouldn't be as much luggage because the Olim who were able would be directed to carry their own bags, there were still scores who needed help. These bags were a nightmare. And now we only had a handful of men, because many had stayed back in Odessa. The women would have to chip in even more.

After the meeting, Roman and I got some fresh air, which helped ease our minds about the next day. We'd get through it just as we did everything else—with the Lord's help. After a brief walk under the stars, we turned in for the night, knowing how important our rest would be.

Fourth Day of Sailing

The morning announcements told us that we'd be arriving in Haifa around five that evening. This would work out great for us, as we'd planned to visit with Shaul, a Jewish man we'd met on our base in Odessa. He had been returning home after a year in Russia working for the Suchnot Agency, a division of the Israeli government that helps young Russian Jews to further their education in Israel. He was about to sail back to Haifa as one of Ebenezer's guests. We'd had dinner with him and told him of our upcoming trip. He graciously told us that he'd pick us up and take us to his house so that we could visit with him and is wife, Yael, during our 24-hour layover.

About mid-day, we had a farewell gathering in the dining room. The waiters served the Olim apple juice in champagne glasses, which delighted them. We sang the Hatikvah, Israel's national anthem, and a few other Hebrew songs. This was right out of Scripture: "...and the ransomed of the Lord shall return, and come to Zion with singing" (Isaiah 35:10). Roman was picked to share his testimony, and one of the leaders shared scriptures about the Olim's returning to Israel. Then Shirley, who led the volunteers on the ship, explained the offloading process to the Olim. She told them that because the volunteers were so few, the Olim would be responsible for getting their own luggage down the gangplank. The volunteers would assist the invalids and disabled people only.

When the meeting finished, the volunteers went through the crowd hugging, kissing, and shaking hands. Roman and I were of the same heart, simultaneously wiping tears from our faces. One woman we had picked up at the Odessa train station came up and handed me a small, inlaid picture framed in birch bark. She had signed the back, having nothing else to give away. A young girl of about ten gave me a flower broach made of cloth and gave Roman a key chain. We told her we would treasure them forever. God's people were practically home. We would never forget this work and never forget these faces.

We docked in Haifa right on time, at five. The gangplank filled with Olim struggling with their bags. I don't think they realized how heavy they were. It was difficult to watch, but we were having a hard time ourselves with the luggage we were responsible for.

At one point Roman and another volunteer were called to help an elderly babushka. The ship's doctor was in her cabin and had given her an IV. An Israeli ambulance driver had come aboard and was also there. Roman and the other volunteer gently lifted her out of the bunk and into the wheelchair. Roman wheeled her out of the cabin to the gangplank. There was a flight of stairs to the dock below. Roman positioned himself, grabbed the bottom of the wheelchair, and hoisted it. The Israeli ambulance driver had the top, the other volunteer held the IV. Step by step, they very carefully made their way down to the waiting ambulance. During the next half hour, Roman repeated this with three more invalids.

The last woman Roman helped down the steps grabbed his hand, kissed it, and wouldn't let go. In a husky voice, Roman told her, "You are home. You are safe." Then he broke down, overcome with the precision with which he was walking out Isaiah's prophecy: "Behold, I will lift My hand in an oath to the nations...they shall bring your sons in their arms, and your daughters shall be carried on their shoulders" (Isaiah 49:22).

By 7:30 we were finished, sweaty, and tired. Every one of the Olim had disembarked and had been processed into the country. The immigration process in Israel, unlike Ukraine, is swift, which was an encouraging introduction for the Olim. They were now either waiting for relatives or being counseled by the Ministry of Absorption, an agency that helps get the Olim transported, settled, and acclimated.

Back on the ship we showered and packed a small overnight bag, as we had planned to spend the evening with Shaul and his wife. True to

Arriving at Haifa Port

Roman helping carry Olim to an ambulance

his word, when we passed through Customs, there he was, all smiles. We hadn't contacted him since the night we met on the base. He had a heart for Ebenezer's ministry, and he had gotten all the information about the ship's embarkation ahead of time, allowing for the offloading of all the Olim.

The Haifa port sits at the base of Mt. Carmel, and Shaul wanted us to see the city from the mountain. So before taking us to his house, he drove us to the top. We stopped at a park that Shaul said had been built with funding from a local church. Even at night, we had a commanding view of Haifa and the surrounding countryside, including lower Galilee. The shine and twinkle of lights beneath us mirrored the stars above, as if we were sandwiched between two skies. The Lord was blessing us yet again, beyond anything we could have asked or thought (Ephesians 3:20).

We continued on to Shaul's house in Qiryat Tivon, a town about thirty minutes away. His wife, Yael, had a beautiful spread of food waiting for us. I was overwhelmed by these people, who we barely knew, so graciously opening their home to us.

We had a wonderful conversation over our meal and continued talking until about 1:30 in the morning. We learned that Shaul and Yael had three sons. Two were in the Israeli Reserves (as was Shaul), and the youngest, seventeen, was away on a school trip. Shaul was a very wise man with a big Jewish heart. He knew his people and knew his land. Roman and I could have listened to him forever. But we had to be back on the ship by 1 P.M. the following day, so we were shown to our bedroom and were asleep in minutes.

The next morning Shaul's TV was on, tuned to CNN. It had only been months, but it seemed like years since we had watched television or heard any real news. The anchor's words, spoken in English, fell over us like spring rain. We sat on the floor, about three feet from the screen, as if we were afraid it would sprout legs and run away. We were transfixed, like two children. A bowl of popcorn was the only thing missing. When we found out the Yankees had clinched the World Series in a sweep over the Padres, we both lifted our arms in the air with a big, "Woo-hoo! Go, Yankees!"

At that moment, Shaul walked into the room. The soft smile on his face told us that he knew exactly how and what we were feeling. He was becoming more familiar with Ebenezer's ministry and understood the sacrifice of its volunteers. Just one day of civilization had brought to the forefront all that we had left behind. We struggled with the thought of returning to time-warped Ukraine. But, as it always did, the knowing that there were more of God's people that needed to be returned to this land triumphed. And we got our few belongings together to head for the port.

On the way to the ship, Shaul had to drop Yael off at Technion University, where she worked in administration. We had a little time after we said our goodbyes to her, and Shaul wanted to show us around a bit. He said he wanted us to be aware of what the Olim could expect when they got there. He wanted us to have first-hand information for our next fishing trip. So while we were there, he showed us around the university, which was comparable to an ivy league back home. Then he brought us to an adult community center, typical of where many of the elderly Olim would wind up. It was a beautiful, modern building, lushly landscaped, with flowers still in bloom. Shaul spoke with the director, who allowed us to walk around and take pictures. The place was clean, well-run, and full of natural light. A far cry from the gray, cement slabs in Odessa.

Next he took us to a nearby shopping center. It was very modern, complete with underground parking. It reminded me so much of home, as did everything we'd experienced there—Haifa's beauty, Shaul and Yael's home, the wonderful food, the television, the college, the senior center. My thoughts of home were intertwined with longing for my children, wondering how they were and how their hearts were holding up. When this yearning took hold, it was powerful, easily able to incapacitate me. As we were getting out of the car, I took a deep breath and silently asked, "Help me." As soon as I did, the yearning subsided with the now familiar assurance deep in my spirit: "*I will take care of your children, as you take care of mine.*"

We followed Shaul to a spot in the mall, just beneath its glass roof, where a scud missile had crashed through, causing extensive damage. Shaul said the Iraqis were trying to strike an oil refinery about two miles away. Thankfully, the missile hit at night when the mall was closed, and it had never exploded. As a memorial, the Israelis had placed an inscribed pillar at the spot the missile had struck.

Our final stop was to a memorial, right in Shaul's town of Tivon, dedicated to the Israeli soldiers in this town who had lost their lives fighting for Israeli independence. It was a very tall, triangular-shaped monument that you could walk inside. On its metallic walls were the names of all the fallen soldiers from Tivon. Alongside the walls were tables with albums that contained a picture of each soldier, along with their names, ages, and other personal information. They were young, handsome men, like our Roman and Keith.

As we were flipping through the albums, Shaul reached into his pants pocket and pulled out a handkerchief. Out of the corner of my eye I saw him catch a tear just before it fell onto the smiling face of a uniformed soldier. This young man could have been any one of his sons. We felt his heart and could imagine only in a small way what he, as an Israeli, knew first hand. These people possessed a transcendent love for their land, a love that had been etched into their DNA through Abraham, Isaac, and Jacob.

Our last few hours in Israel had been spent so wisely. Thanks to Shaul, we got a flavor for this country that we never otherwise would have had and could now share first hand with our next group of Olim. This unexpected and unanticipated blessing was one more confirmation that the Lord continued to go before us.

At the port, we thanked and blessed Shaul, knowing we had made a lifelong friend and that we would see him again. We cleared customs and boarded the ship in time for lunch. The ship was late disembarking and left the Haifa port for Odessa at around 3:30.

It would take us three days to return to Odessa. The ship was practically empty, with only about fifty to sixty passengers. The ship sells tickets on the return voyage, and many of the Olim in Israel use these trips to visit their families in Ukraine. We met several Olim who had made Aliyah on prior Ebenezer sailings and were going back for a visit after having lived in Israel a few years. Speaking with them was refreshing and encouraging. They admitted that it was very hard for them to assimilate, that the adjustment had been difficult. But, in the end, their stories were always positive, testaments to what Israel had to offer.

It had only been a little over a day since we had handled the luggage and since Roman had carried those women in their wheelchairs. We were still tired and sore. It never ceased to amaze me how the Lord worked it out so that every time we extended ourselves to the max, on the wings of it, there were opportunities to rest. And that is exactly what Roman and I did during those next three days.

During the trip, we had our usual morning and evening worship and prayer time, but other than that, we really had no responsibilities. We got a chance to enjoy the ship, taking advantage of things like the inexpensive but excellent cappuccinos in the Veranda Bar on the upper deck. I'd never had one, believe it or not, until this sailing. It completely spoiled me, especially when compared to the weak coffee I made on the base.

Roman got a special treat when we were invited by the captain to have a tour of the bridge. I didn't understand much of what I was told or saw, but Roman did. He's always been intrigued by instruments and equipment, and these were definitely state-of-the-art. The ship had satellite positioning, surface radar, and no wheel, just a small yoke that aided in steering. Two men were constantly on watch, monitoring it all, but the ship ran on autopilot. I was thankful that Roman was treated to this. It really lifted his spirits.

It was like being on a honeymoon. We enjoyed the sun, the sea, and especially the sunsets. But like their very essence, sunsets are reflective. And with each sunset came the ache for my children, for home. The tug-of-war between this work and our kids and our lives back home would be one from which Roman and I would never escape.

On our second night, we went through the Bosphorous Straights. Roman and I were positioned at our favorite spot on the bow to take in the sight of Istanbul. As beautiful as it had been in the daytime, it was just as magnificent in the evening. The mosques were aflame with light, golden against the dark hillsides. There were scores of boats in the area, all lit up as well. Because the Straits are so narrow, the ship moved very slowly. Roman and I went up to the top deck above the bridge to get an even better view. Just as we got there, the ship sounded a long blast of its horn.

Straight ahead, on an intersecting course with our ship, was another boat. We were on a 10,000-ton ship. What headed directly toward us was a fishing boat, maybe eight to ten tons. In the Straits, with all the other ships, there was little room for us to navigate and not much more for the fishing boat. Roman and I immediately thought of Paul in the book of Acts and how he sailed on these same waters and got shipwrecked on the island of Malta. As the boat got closer, Roman and I grabbed the railing and prayed, experiencing a measure of the fear we were sure Paul must have felt.

Just when it looked like the boat was going to ram our stern, it passed—and I mean *just* passed—across our path. When my heartbeat returned to normal, I was able to sense in my spirit that this was part of the backlash we should come to expect in this work. Sure enough, on the other side of the Bosphorous Straits, as we entered the Black Sea, as we got closer to bringing more of God's people home, the water began to churn.

Chapter 10 ❧

More Fishing

I will keep You and give You as a covenant to the people, as a light
to the Gentiles, to open blind eyes, to bring out prisoners from the
prison, those who sit in darkness from the prison house.
—Isaiah 42:6–7

THE FIRST TIME I felt any seasickness was the last day of our trip.
From the moment we entered the Black Sea, the swells had been constant
and at about twelve feet high. When we arrived at the Odessa port, I was
unstable and queasy. Roman, however, was fine. He became exhilarated,
in fact, when we pulled into the dock. Right next to us was the *U.S.S.*
Austin, an amphibious assault ship that carried Marine helicopters. It
was part of the Marine's sixth fleet, with one missile frigate and four
destroyer escorts. As I said before, this was the type of thing, like touring
the ship's bridge, that excited Roman and filled him with a childlike
awe. And again, I thanked the Lord for His grace over Roman, for giving
him these special treats.

We passed through customs and were met by two of the Russian
volunteers. I still felt a little dizzy and shaky, but it did feel good to be
home again. How strange it was that Odessa had become home.

When we got to the base, we were given the emails that had come
in while we were away. We were thrilled, but waited to get settled in our
room before feasting on them. Unfortunately, the room we'd had before

we left, the one with the precious private bathroom, had been given away. When volunteers sail, their rooms have to be completely emptied. So before we left, we had to pack everything and keep whatever we weren't taking on the ship in the base's storage area. There were guests on the base from time to time, and our room had been given to one of them. The packing, unpacking, and adjusting to new accommodations was part and parcel of what we had to continually deal with. It was just one aspect of the breaking the Lord was doing in us.

Our new room was in the corpus. I had dreaded ever having to live in this facility. It was shoddy, dirty, and smelly. There were community baths and toilets. The sinks leaked onto the floor. The toilets didn't always flush. The rooms were really small, and the beds were lumpy. We had been spoiled by the extravagance of the ship. Our room had been small, but at least it was private, with our own bath. I'd had enough communal living after being on our fishing trip. I longed for my privacy again.

Our room was at the very end of a hallway. It was much too small for two people, but we'd have to manage. To our surprise, there was a small sink tucked in a corner and a small half refrigerator. But both looked as if they hadn't been used or cleaned in years. Similarly, the walls screamed from neglect, appearing gray from a lack of paint. Worn, yellowing curtains hung like limp rags from rusted curtain rods. When we sat on the two single beds, we sank to the middle. The room was representative of the heart of this nation, not only towards its infrastructure but also, as we'd continue to find out on our upcoming fishing trip, towards its people.

We unpacked only a few things, toiletries mostly, as there wasn't room for much. There was only a small table with one chair and a small closet. For our time in that room, we decided to live out of our suitcases. Besides, we knew we'd be moving again one or two times before our term was up.

As Roman scrubbed the sink, I could smell the water. It reminded me of rotten eggs. And it had a brownish, rusty color. The fridge smelled moldy, so we cleaned it out as best we could and plugged it in, hoping running it would help.

We got water from the bathroom down the hall to make instant coffee in our electric kettle—I again thanked God that I had brought it from the States. Then we settled down to devour our emails. How strange and disconcerting it was to be halfway across the world with the only connection to our seed being words on a page. It was eerie and felt hollow, giving rise to regret. Had we done the right thing? Were we bad parents? Then Roman, my dear, sweet, faithful Roman, broke my reverie.

"Come on, Babe. Let's get some shut-eye. The Lord's people need us again tomorrow."

The five days before the next sailing were a carbon copy of the week before our trip to Haifa. Every day we got up well before dawn, picked up more Olim, and handled more luggage. It seemed like no sooner had we healed and rested from the last sailing than we were back at it all over again.

I can't overemphasize how strenuous this work was. So much so that the volunteers began having to take a day off out of every two or three, especially the women. On one of my days off, I tried to sleep in while Roman got himself ready. The power was out that morning, so he got dressed by candlelight and flashlight. Even with light, you couldn't move in that room without bumping into something, and it sounded like Roman was banging into everything. It's a wonder we didn't kill ourselves in that room. I had strung a clothesline across the room because I had planned to do wash that day, Odessa style—by hand, with cold water, in the bathroom sink—and I was afraid Roman would catch himself in it. With all the commotion, I gave up trying to sleep

Looking back as I write this, it sounds comical. But at the time, life there was so frustrating that it often brought me to tears. The weather had become cold and damp, so any clothes I washed would take days to dry. And we couldn't wash our jeans at all, because they were too thick to do by hand and couldn't be wrung out. So we just brushed the dust and mud off them. And I was always cold, something I dread, because it takes forever for me to warm up again. The heat in our room was intermittent, if at all.

I missed home so much sometimes. I missed my washing machine, having heat all day, having lights and a television and a newspaper. I missed having a real cup of coffee. When this discouragement came upon me, I realized what I had taken for granted. The Russians had no problem with any of this because they didn't know anything else.

After Roman got himself off, I hand washed some laundry and then tried to get a few emails out. But once again, after writing for half an hour, the power went out. Everything in me just wanted to run away. Nothing worked. Nothing was easy. Nothing was normal. This culture stripped you of everything, inside and out. I knew the Lord was working in us, but I didn't want Him to do any more in me. We were only half way through our time in Ukraine, and I felt as if I had had it.

As I made my way back to the room, craving a cup of coffee that I knew I couldn't have, I came across some of the children who would be sailing in a few days. They giggled and smiled and tried to speak with me. I couldn't understand what they were saying, of course, but their joy was like a shot of B-12. The heaviness immediately lifted and I found myself giggling and smiling right along with them. This was what I needed—not lights, not a washing machine, not a cup of coffee. I needed a reminder of why the Lord had called us there. And through these children, He had gently tapped me on the shoulder.

The night before sailing day we had our usual preparation meeting. We were informed that there would be almost four hundred Olim on this trip, more than any of the other sailings. The only thing Roman and I could think about was the bags.

Sailing day dawned. Again, we arrived at the Odessa port. Again, right alongside the steps to the port building was a perfectly good escalator. Again, we were not allowed to use it. Again, the men formed a human chain from the buses to the stairs and up to the building. There were many more elderly on this sailing. Most were weak, walked with canes, and needed assistance up the scores of steps to the second floor.

I, along with several other women, struggled with the baggage-laden trolleys. The wind blew them from side to side while pelting sand and a salty mist into our faces. We weren't allowed to bring the trolleys onto the ship—the captain said it would damage the carpet. So again, like human mules, the men, who were by now well-trained, did all the work. From the gangplank they offloaded the bags and carried them on their backs onto the ship. It was warm on the ship, and they were heavily dressed, both for the weather and to protect their backs from the weight of the luggage. By the time they delivered the bags and came down the gangplank to get more, they were drenched in sweat.

Again, we saw hundreds of Olim off from the port. We cheered, sang songs, and waved the Israeli flag. This spectacle of God's prophetic hand at work, witnessing His bringing His people home, brought new life to our weary bodies. It was as if the Lord Himself were saying to our aching bones, "Surely I will cause breath to enter into you, and you shall live" (Ezekiel 37:5).

The ship sailed on Friday. By the end of the weekend, we were fairly well rested, which was a good thing, because Monday morning we began our second fishing trip to Odessa's surrounding areas. We'd be making day trips, returning to the base at night. During the next ten days, we were to visit twenty-five families.

Now experienced fishermen, Roman and I were familiar with the process and thought that we knew what to expect. But no matter how well-prepared we thought we were, the reality of life in Ukraine slammed us afresh every time.

One of the first homes we visited was that of a man named Leonid, a diabetic who gave himself injections. He had a daughter, but she wasn't around. He was attentive to everything we told him about Ebenezer and making Aliyah to Israel. Then, through the translator, he told us his family's story.

His grandfather was a rabbi during World War II. He and some other Jews were thrown into a cattle car by Nazi soldiers, who poured gasoline over them and burned them alive.

His daughter was married, with one son. A few years before in Russia, she had been seriously injured in a ferry-boat accident. The ferry collided with a railroad bridge. The force of the impact derailed a freight train, toppling its cars onto the ferry and sinking it. His daughter survived, but she sustained a severe head injury that peeled her skull away like a banana. He said she now suffered from constant headaches and dizziness.

After we shared the Scriptures with him, he said through the translator, "I sense a real presence of God in this flat." Then he said he wanted to go to Israel. Here it was again, prophecy being fulfilled right before our eyes: "And you will be gathered up one by one, O you children of Israel" (Isaiah 27:12).

Another family we visited early on was a widow and her twenty-four-year-old daughter, who had cerebral palsy. As the translator talked with the mother, I looked around the room.

The flat was small, dirty, and congested, not unlike many others we had visited. But for some reason the level of poverty and hopelessness screamed louder here. Maybe because of the daughter, who was lying lifelessly on the bed. I thought of my own daughter and could not imagine what this mother's heart had to endure.

I had an overwhelming feeling that no one ever came here, that they never got out. I didn't see a wheelchair anywhere, but I wanted to get the girl outside for some fresh air. I wanted to make them a good meal. I wanted to stay and clean the apartment. But I had to ask the Lord to help me keep myself in check. And somehow, deep inside, I knew, really knew, that the girl could hear and understand what the translator was saying about Ebenezer and the hope of Israel. I knew that Jesus saw beyond the limp body lying on that bed. I knew that He died as much for this girl as He did for every one of us.

As this knowing began to ease my heart, the mother motioned us to come near her daughter's bed. The young woman began to speak, but so softly and with such effort that we had to bend down to hear the words. They were in Russian, then translated: "God must have sent you to us." We told the girl, "He did."

More than anything, it was these fishing trips that changed us from the inside out. It was on this ground, in the everyday lives and problems of these people, that we saw the hand of the Lord. It was here, going from house to house like the apostles, that we were captured and held by a love beyond our comprehension. And in it I felt fully alive, doing something that caused every part of me to work as a complete whole and in complete harmony. As heartbreaking as these visits were, as desperately as I missed my children, I knew this love for His people would be my calling forever.

Before we left this flat, we gathered around the bed with the mother and knelt beside the girl. I wrapped her bony hands in mine, and we all prayed to the God of Israel. We asked for favor over this family and that He would make a way for the mother to find the money and time to do all that was necessary to get their paperwork in order. Although Ebenezer would help, I couldn't see how she would be able to leave her daughter to stand in the lines and visit the agencies that she'd need to. But I wasn't supposed to understand it, just believe what He promised in Isaiah 45:2: "I will go before you and make the crooked places straight; I will break in pieces the gates of bronze and cut the bars of iron."

Later that same day, we walked into another seemingly hopeless situation. The apartment building we were visiting was in desperate shape, filled with that smell that made me nauseous. A middle-aged man, his demeanor shouting defeat, greeted us at a splintering door. We followed him into the living area. His wife sat across the room in a wheelchair.

The translator shared about our work and why we were there. Then the man told us that he was caring for his twelve-year-old grandson because his daughter had no food for him. The man had been working, but he hadn't been paid in seven months. As he spoke, something pulled my gaze toward his wife.

She didn't appear to be paying attention to what was happening, as if she were in another world. Then I looked down and was shocked to see that she had a foot missing. It must have been amputated recently, because there was a clear bandage wrapped around the bottom of her leg.

It was oozing fresh blood. She had a paper bag next to her chair and a bowl on her lap. She was snapping off the heads of sardines, pulling the intestines out and dropping them in the paper bag. Then she dropped the fish, what was left of it, into the bowl. I couldn't imagine that all that effort would feed even one person.

With the smell, the woman's condition, and my waning spirit, I had to fight hard not to run out of there, not to scream from disgust and disbelief. This culture was so hard to be in! Yet, never before had the Lord drawn us so closely to His side. Without Him, without His fortitude, there was no way any one of us could have continued on.

We prayed for this family, knowing how much they would benefit from moving to Israel and that only the Lord would be able to make it happen.

Another couple we visited that day was elderly, the wife disabled. She was totally immobile and had been bedridden for ten months with a broken hip. Her husband had been caring for her. I couldn't comprehend this—how a person could lie in bed for ten months and do nothing. In the States, a hip replacement is a common procedure. I knew if she stayed in Ukraine, she'd probably never walk.

Again, the frustration at this systemic sickness began to take hold. I felt as if, with each family, it was slowly creeping up my legs, just waiting for the right moment to grab hold of my heart and squeeze. This was a minute-by-minute battle. I had to draw continually upon the Lord's Word, His promises. I had to discern continually when it was time to "stand still, and see the salvation of the Lord" (Exodus 14:13). I had to keep reminding myself that "the battle is the Lord's" (1 Samuel 17:47), not mine.

Even though we told the husband about the medical help his wife could get in Israel, he didn't want to move his wife, and he wouldn't even consider leaving for Israel at this time. We understood how impossible the relocation seemed to this man, but we knew we served a mighty God. We prayed with this couple and left a food parcel with them.

Depending on how the trips had been set up, some days we'd visit three or four families and other days we would visit twice that many. And just when we thought we'd seen the worst, the Lord would show us otherwise.

There was an apartment building in Odessa that I truly could not believe was inhabited. The others we'd been to, both on this trip and in Kirovograd, had been horrible, worse than we'd ever seen in our lives. But the building we drove up to this particular morning sent shivers down my spine.

We entered a long, dark hallway. I pulled my turtleneck up to avoid the smell of urine. The lights were out again, so we had to use our flashlights. Cigarette buts, scrunched candy wrappers, empty beer cans, and vodka bottles littered the floor. The stairs, too, as we made our way up to the apartment, were filled with junk.

We knocked on the door and were met by a stout, middle-aged woman clothed, literally, in rags. Every section of her oversized dress was ripped and torn. The filth and poverty inside was evident, even through the partially opened door. She welcomed us inside and showed us to some wooden chairs. Again, looking around, I had the urge to bolt from my chair and begin scrubbing. Everything from the walls to the floor to the cabinets to every viewable surface was covered in a layer of what looked like yellow grease.

After we shared with her about the God of Israel wanting to return her and her family to Israel, she shared her story. She said that her thirty-three-year-old daughter, also dressed in rags and sitting in a chair across the room, was mentally disabled and had to be watched constantly. When the daughter was a year old, she had received a polio vaccine. Something went wrong with the serum or syringe, damaging her for life.

This poor young woman desperately needed a bath. Her hair looked like it had never been combed. How backward and foreign this culture was to me. In the States, there were agencies to help with this kind of handicap. Back home, she'd be a functioning person.

As the mother spoke, we noticed that there was a deep, open sore the size of a quarter on her nose. It was probably leprosy, and not surprising, considering the filth around us. She told us that she had been sick for the past seven months. I didn't want to know from what. I was beginning to get scared for our own health. I had to force myself to trust that we were in the hands of Almighty God and that He would protect us. As

Psalm 91:7 says, "A thousand may fall at your side, and ten thousand at your right hand; but it shall not come near you."

The woman didn't seem open to going to Israel, which amazed me in light of the way she was living. We prayed with her and left a food parcel, for which she was extremely thankful.

By the time we got outside, I was gasping for air. Again, the smells seemed to attach to my clothes, and I was feeling nauseous. I knew I would never, ever forget these smells. We stood outside the van for a few minutes, taking in the air before heading to our next stop.

When we arrived, we were greeted by an elderly woman with a lovely countenance. Her apartment, though very small, thankfully didn't have the strong odor of the previous one. The woman was very receptive as we shared Ebenezer's work with her and told her about what the God of Israel was doing to bring His people back to the land.

She shared through the translator that during the war she had suffered some sort of concussion that had resulted in headaches ever since. She had them every day. When she told us this, something inside moved me to minister to her. This stirring hadn't happened before, at least not in such a strong way. I didn't know what to do, but finally I stepped out in faith, telling the translator that I needed to pray for the woman. I walked over to the bed she was sitting on and placed my hands on her head. I prayed a short prayer in English for her healing. Then the translator continued to explain about Ebenezer's work.

As we were making our way out of the apartment, the woman told us that her headache was gone and that she wanted to go to Israel. We told her that the God of Israel loved her and that we did also. We embraced her and left a food parcel for her. This visit made up for the last. That's how the Lord worked with us. As soon as we got discouraged, He'd lift us right back up.

Another stop that day was to the home of a middle-aged man who was paralyzed. When we knocked on the door, he called us inside from his bed. He lived in a one-room flat. There were a set of weights attached to his bed that looked like they dated back to the war. He was smiling, as if he had accepted his fate.

He listened attentively to the hopeful news we brought. Amazingly, in his condition, he seemed receptive. But in Israel, the law requires that

The woman I prayed for

invalids have someone to care for them. And this man had no relatives living there. We had to remember, though, that our God is bigger than laws, and we were just there to deliver His message.

Little by little, visit by visit, we were gaining a new perspective, looking beyond what we saw with our eyes. We had come too far, seen and experienced too much, to limit the Lord. This man's legs were broken, but his heart wasn't. God had a plan for him. "For I know the thoughts that I think toward you…thoughts of peace and not of evil, to give you a future and a hope" (Jeremiah 29:11).

In any given day, by the fourth or fifth visit, I was poured out. It was hard to convey this to the Russians on the team, as they had become hardened to the life-draining need that smothered us. I stayed close to Roman, leaning on him more than just physically. He'd always encourage me to be sensitive to my limits, suggesting from time to time that I stay behind in the van. But I wanted to be with him every second. He was immersed in this ministry, his whole being fed by his passion for the Lord's people. That is what gave me strength—watching him share, hearing him speak prophecy over these people, and knowing what he had left behind to do it.

Our fifth stop was to the home of a woman who we found out was only sixty, but who looked ninety. This was another deplorable situation, where garbage was strewn from one end of the apartment to the other. The woman wasn't friendly at all. After she heard our message, she was adamant about not going to Israel. Through the translator, it sounded like she had received some misinformation. But even so, it was incomprehensible to me to see these people in their hopeless situations not wanting something better.

Before we left, we asked if we could pray for her. She said, "Not if you pray like they do at the synagogue." We assured her we wouldn't, and we just said a few simple prayers. As we did, we sensed the Lord, the love of Jesus, very strongly over this woman. I knew she'd never experienced anything like the way we were ministering to her at that moment.

When we were ready to leave, we gave her a food parcel. Then she told us that she'd think about making Aliyah. This complete reversal again brought to life God's very words through Ezekiel: "I will give you a new heart and put a new spirit within you; I will take the heart of stone out of your flesh and give you a heart of flesh. I will put My Spirit within you and cause you to walk in My statutes..." (Ezekiel 36:26–27).

Our sixth stop was to a building that was, unbelievably, in worse shape than any of the others. It was as if the Lord was telling us not to think we'd seen the worst until He told us that we had.

We were all afraid to enter this building. It was dark, so we had to use our flashlights. The stairwell was shored up only by birch logs that were about a foot in diameter. The woman we were to visit was on the third floor, which was at the top. Another woman, named Vera, who was affiliated with Ebenezer, met us when we arrived. She would be the local contact for the woman we were about to visit, who apparently was elderly and disabled.

The stairs truly looked like they wouldn't hold our weight. Roman suggested that we go up one at a time, which is what we did. Carefully mounting each step, we used our flashlights to secure our footing. I'm sure that those who knew the Lord were once again repeating, as I was, Philippians 4:13: "I can do all things through Christ who strengthens me."

We finally got to the top and made our way down the hall. As we did, I began to get nauseous. There was that horrid smell again. I couldn't understand what could possibly produce something so foul. I will never forget it as long as I live.

We found the apartment and knocked on the door. It opened by itself. We made our way inside a tiny foyer, pulled forward by a small light in a room up ahead. We found an old lady named Zoya, who was probably in her eighties, sitting alone in a corner on a mattress. She gave us a big smile and was so happy that we had made it to her apartment. She reminded me of a lost puppy. I immediately wanted to take her home, clean her up, and take care of her.

We shared the news of Aliyah with Zoya. She was alert and listened to everything we said. As the translator was speaking, I motioned to her, trying not to scream. A roach was crawling up the sleeve of her sweater. She screamed, swatting the bug off with her hand.

Zoya said she'd like to go to Israel, but that she had no relatives there. Again, this would pose a problem, as the elderly and disabled are supposed to have family with them. She told us that her daughter, who wanted her apartment, had her passport and wouldn't relinquish it until Zoya turned the apartment over to her. We, of course, suggested she do this. Then we prayed with her and left a food parcel and all of the information she needed to get started with the relocation process. Vera was with us the whole time and said she would speak with Zoya's daughter. Maybe she could convince her to accompany her mother to Israel.

These people, especially the sick, elderly, and disabled who were saying "yes" to Aliyah, were living testaments to the Lord's goodness and His faithfulness to His people. Just as His Word says in Isaiah 42:22, we were witnessing "...a people robbed and plundered...snared in holes." And He was saying "...to the north, 'Give them up!'... Bring My sons from afar and My daughters from the ends of the earth" (Isaiah 43:6). And as humbled, awed, and grateful as I was to have been called and picked to do this work, its weight was cumulative.

After days like this one, I wanted to run home for some rest and a good, hot meal. I wanted to share my heart with my friends. I thought about my children and wondered if they would ever understand what was happening to us here. How could anyone understand what this work does to the insides of a person? It was beginning to grip me as if attaching itself to my womb. And when we'd get back to the base, I'd feel dirty all over, unable to get rid of the smells. Many nights there was no hot water. And I'd just cry. Like Dorothy, I wanted to fall asleep and wake up and be back home—back in my own house with hot showers, hot coffee, and my kids. Instead, we'd wash as best we could in our rust-stained sink and have a late dinner.

Caving into our flimsy mattresses, our bodies, minds, and spirits felt as if they'd been tossed, turned, and slammed.

About half way through our ten-day fishing assignment, we had another unforgettable day. One of our stops was at an apartment complex that was surrounded by steel doors that had to be opened from the inside.

Zoya's apartment building

Zoya!

We hadn't been forewarned about this, so we just stood outside the doors, asking the Lord to intervene. In a few minutes, a woman came out and we were able to go inside—and coming down a flight of stairs was the very woman we were scheduled to meet walking with her friend.

We introduced ourselves and then found a couple of halfway decent benches outside. The woman was excited to see us, saying that she had been housebound for two years. She'd just had some sort of surgery and this was her first day venturing out. We praised the Lord for her recovery. After we shared the news of Aliyah, she was ready and willing to go. We prayed with her and her friend, who promised to help the woman get her documents.

These were the types of visits that spoke life into us. As I've said before, we needed these to balance the others, especially the particularly heart-wrenching ones, like our last visit that day. Again, the Lord seemed to be warning us not to think we'd seen the worst until He'd told us we had.

The family lived in an apartment complex that seemed to stretch for miles. One building was a carbon copy of the next. We finally found our apartment, the outside of which looked as horrible as all the others. The inside, however, was worse. There had been a fire in this flat, and you could still smell the smoke. This was a family of six—mother, father, two daughters, and two granddaughters. Through the translator, the mother told us that the fire trucks had arrived, but there was no water; it had been turned off. This family lived out the cliché we so haphazardly use back home—they had watched everything they owned go up in smoke.

Looking around, it seemed like they had moved right back in after the fire had been put out. The walls were black. Except for two mattresses on the floor, there was no furniture. All their bedding, blankets, and clothing had been destroyed. While the translator was speaking with the mother, I looked over at the two little girls. Both wore short-sleeved, summer dresses. I got chills just looking at them. The weather had turned freezing, and we were all layered with warm clothing. The state had promised to provide aid, but it had been two months, and none had come.

We told this family about the work of Ebenezer and shared the Scriptures with them. As we did, I noticed, sitting on a charred table,

Fire-damaged apartment

Our team with the family of six who lived there

a small Torah that was in good condition. Later, the woman confirmed that the Torah had been the only item untouched by the fire. We knew that the Lord had gone before us here, and we determined to do everything we could to help these people. We left two food parcels and all the information about making Aliyah. We told them that we would come back in a few days with aid. On the base we had a storage area where we kept boxes of clothes, coats, and shoes donated from other countries. And humanitarian aid shipments came every few months from overseas.

That night, as we headed back to the base, the van was filled with hope and expectation as we talked about returning with the items this family so desperately needed.

On our last day of fishing, we visited four families. The first lived in a small house on the outskirts of Odessa. An elderly lady named Roza greeted us. She was putting several pairs of old shoes into a bag, hoping to sell them so she could buy some food. She was a widow with a monthly pension of thirty grivnya, the equivalent of six American dollars. She said her gas bill was more than that. She continued, through the translator, telling us that she had a daughter who had committed suicide. She also had a forty-four-year-old son and a twenty-three-year-old granddaughter.

We shared the Scriptures with her and told her of the hope of Israel. She had a desire to leave but said that all of her documents had been destroyed in the war. We assured her that Ebenezer would help her to recreate her paperwork. She said she'd speak to her son about it. The food parcel we left brought her to tears.

On our second visit, we met Nena, a younger woman, probably in her fifties, whose husband had died only six months before. Like Roza, Nena's pension was meager—forty-six grivnya, or about nine American dollars, barely enough to provide bread for a month.

After we shared the work of Ebenezer and the Scriptures with her, Nena told us her situation. Her two sons were studying at the university to avoid the draft. She had considered relocating to Germany, as they offered immigration to Jews as a sort of restitution. She said she'd be open to making Aliyah after her sons finished school in another year. She said she had her birth certificate, which would be a huge help when applying for her documents. We urged her not to wait and to apply as soon as possible. This was an encouraging visit. I couldn't understand how these widows survived; the country had nothing in place for its people.

Our third visit was to an elderly woman who lived alone. She was partially blind and hard of hearing. She told us that she was very involved with the Jewish community and in the local synagogue, and she was proud that she spoke Hebrew. She had no interest in going to Israel, saying that Ukraine was her mother land and she wanted to be buried there with all her relatives. (Again, there was the tie to the dead.) We knew that "…a remnant of them will return" (Isaiah 10:22) and that if her heart was going to change, only the Lord could do it.

Our fourth and final stop was to see a family of three—a grandmother, a daughter, and a granddaughter. The grandmother was lying in bed when we arrived. She'd had two strokes and seemed very ill. The daughter said she was a scientist and was currently working. In Ukraine, sophisticated names were often given to jobs that don't warrant them. We assumed this woman probably majored in science in college and was doing some medical work. She said she was afraid that if she went to Israel, she'd have to start at the bottom. She told us that her present job was very good and her career was moving along. Seeing what I had so far, I couldn't imagine what sort of career that was. But for the sake of the future of this woman's daughter, we encouraged her with the Scriptures, making sure she understood that it was her God calling her home, not us.

Once our fishing trip was over, we had another week of pick-ups at the train station and another sailing to prepare for. There would be two additional sailings we'd be involved with before our term here was up. Then, in about three weeks, Roman and I would sail to Haifa. We were planning to spend two weeks in Israel volunteering at the Christian Friends of Israel. As a special treat, we planned to meet up with Shannon and her husband, Billy, who had arranged to be on a tour during our stay. And then we'd fly home. At this point it seemed like that was an eternity away, especially now that we were facing the balance of the sailings in the dead of the Ukrainian winter. Until you've experienced a Russian winter, you don't know what winter is.

As soon as the weather got really cold, sailing days became even more of a nightmare. I had to pry myself out of bed in the mornings at 5:00, with snowflakes the size of golf balls falling, knowing we'd be facing a breakfast of eggs swimming in grease. I usually just had some bread and hot tea. It wasn't enough fuel for the work we were doing, but I was never one to eat too much in the morning anyway.

At the dock, the wind and the snow made an already horrendous job nearly impossible. Instead of the two women it usually took to push each trolley to the gangplank, it now took three. We had to fight the biting gusts off the Black Sea, as well as the layer of slush that continued to build along the port. Fighting the wind caused us to move at a snail's pace, which exhausted us even more. The cold went right through you, no matter how many layers of clothes you wore. We walked with our heads down, hoods up, and scarves wrapped around our faces, and still the cold took our breath away.

On the port, the men had the worst of it. I could see Roman lifting the bags onto his shoulders, then his back. As with all the men, only his eyes were visible. Their heads, necks, and faces were protectively wrapped. But I could see his eyes squint and then open wide as it took everything within him to gingerly climb those ice-encrusted stairs hauling all that weight. Later he told me that he sometimes thought he wouldn't make it to the top.

How many people would do this? I wondered about our friends back home. Would they have left already? Would this level of physical work have made them pack up? We heard that some volunteers did just that. And I completely understood—I felt like quitting myself many days. The only explanation I have as to why we didn't was the Lord's grace. He kept us safe and somehow kept us going.

Pushing the trolleys on ice

Loading the ship in snow

Between sailings we had some down time. During one of our days off, Roman and I went to a large flea market in Odessa to look for a fur hat for me. It was very crowded, and for a short period Roman and I got separated. I was sandwiched between several people just as I spotted Roman. Then a vendor from one of the booths shouted at us, "Document! Document!" I had forgotten, but one of the volunteers at the base had told me about the pickpockets at the market. My heart dropped as I checked my zipper pocket. It was open, and my passport and money were gone. Roman's had been taken, too. All I could think about was not being able to get out of this country. And I knew what it was like trying to get documents here—next to impossible.

Within a few minutes we found a policeman and told him what happened. A nearby attendant translated. We were told that this was common, that the pickpockets take the passports to look for money between the pages. He said that our passports would probably show up at the Bureau of Information. Knowing this country, we were totally discouraged by that Statement. A hot panic rose inside of me. Those passports were our keys to the States. Without them, what would happen to us? I shook with insecurity, even as I called on the Lord.

As we began walking toward the market's information center, a man approached us. He seemed to come out of nowhere. Without a word, he handed us our passports and walked away. At first we were dumbfounded. But then it began to dawn on us. The whole thing had been staged, a slick sting operation. In this poverty-stricken country, our passports were of no use to them. They just wanted the money, and Americans are easy targets. Everyone probably got something—the policeman, the attendant, and the pickpocket, who could have been the man with our passports. But we were so relieved to have our documents back that we didn't care about anything else.

About a week later, we were picking up families from their homes to bring them to the ship when we were met by another culture shock.

One family lived in a communal residence with a large kitchen area and several small, studio-like apartments off of it. As we were gathering the luggage of the family we were transporting, I noticed a woman in the kitchen boiling a pot of water. There was a small baby on the floor, and I assumed the water was being heated for her bath—this was common there.

As I brought the luggage outside, I glanced up at the window ledges, where bunches of pigeons were landing. All of a sudden, a window opened. The woman who had been boiling the water reached out, grabbed a pigeon by its neck, and dragged it inside. When I told Roman what I'd seen, he wasn't surprised—nothing here seemed to surprise him. Then one of the volunteers who was with us told me that the woman would make pigeon soup and that they bait the birds with crumbs on the window ledges. As we learned with the rancid meat in those sandwiches, these people were creative when it came to eating. And just as they were resourceful with food, we soon found out that they were inventive in other situations too.

One day, a few hours before lunch, the gas on the base went out. The stove in the kitchen ran on gas, so that meant the babushkas couldn't cook. We had over a hundred hungry Olim looking forward to soup and nothing to cook it with.

I went to the kitchen, curious to see how they'd handle this. The babushkas and a few others who helped in the kitchen talked animatedly back and forth in Russian. I couldn't understand anything, so I went back to my room. About forty-five minutes later I went to the office and asked what would be happening for lunch. I was told to go outside. I did, and there, in the freezing cold, was an old babushka, wrapped from head to toe, stirring what looked like a cauldron of soup with a huge, old wooden spoon. The women had made a fire out of some old pieces of wood to keep them warm. Then they found a metal stove, made a fire in it, and put a huge pot of soup on top. There was enough to feed a hundred people. The scene was something out of a World War II movie.

I had picked up quite a few Russian words, and I walked over and asked if I could stir the pot. With a gentle smile, the old babushka handed me the spoon. Roman had come outside with his camera and snapped a picture. How gracious the Lord was; His people would get taken care of no matter what.

Cooking outside

Our time was coming to an end, our final sailing to Haifa only days away. The past three months had sucked the life from us in a way we'd never felt before. Facing this culture and its incomprehensible need had created a vacuum where our sense of normal used to be. Yet, ever since our last fishing trip Roman and I had prayed about returning the next year, in February. As much as we missed our children, our home, and our country, we had become knit to this work. Our hearts had become so connected to these people, we couldn't imagine not coming back, not continuing to do what we felt even more so now that we had been called to do. Particular scriptures began to take hold in our minds: "The harvest truly is plentiful, but the laborers are few" (Matthew 9:37). "I will say to the north, Give them up! And to the south, do not keep them back! Bring My sons from afar and my daughters from the ends of the earth" (Isaiah 43:6).

We asked the base leaders if they could put in a request for us to return. But we were told that the list had already been made up for the following year. We had to rest in knowing that the Lord had control of our lives. He knew how much more work there was to be done. If He wanted us to be a part of it, He'd make a way.

The day before we were to sail to Haifa to spend two weeks and then return home, we were in our room packing when there was a knock on the door. It was two of the base leaders. It was unusual for them to come to our room, and I immediately got scared. What did we do wrong? Was the ship detained? Was our family all right? Then one of them said, "We have good news for you. The leaders in England have considered your names for next year. Not only are you now on the list to return in February, but also they would like you to take leadership positions for your term."

My hand flew to my mouth. We asked how it had happened. "This is the Lord's work," one of them said. "He makes all the adjustments and changes." This was actually the greatest truth we would come to know in a real and living way in the days and years ahead.

As wonderful as the news was, the reality of it brought a slew of new questions. Leaders had pastoral and other responsibilities on the base. How would we do this? We had spent everything we had. Where would the money come from? We hadn't told Keith, Roman Eric, and Shannon that it had been on our hearts to return because we didn't think we'd be able to. How would they take this news? I had to put all of this behind me. It was far beyond the grace I had at the moment. I'd heard many times how, in a moment, the Lord can change your life. Just minutes ago we had been planning to return home to the way of life we had left. And then, suddenly, everything was different.

That night we thanked the Lord together and in our hearts. As joined as we were in this work, we each had our own conflicts about what returning meant. For Roman, it would put him further away from regaining any semblance of the job he had left and further away from being able to provide for his family. For me, it primarily meant a longer separation from my home and my children.

We climbed into bed that last night of our term wrapped in the security blanket of the words spoken earlier: "This is the Lord's work. He makes all the adjustments and changes."

Chapter 11 ∽

Two Weeks
in the Holy Land

And the angel of the Lord came back the second time, and touched him, and said, "Arise and eat, because the journey is too great for you."
—1 Kings 19:7

IN THE THREE months we had been in Odessa, we had taken part in six sailings and helped to return over two thousand of God's children home. Now, after all that and eight hours of loading the ship, we were on board, headed for Israel, our last bout with the luggage behind us until we returned.

We had been anticipating this trip for weeks. We were excited about meeting up with Shannon and Billy, about our stay in Israel, and of course, about finally going home. But our immediate craving was for steamy showers and lean meat.

The past six weeks on the base had been the most difficult of our stay, primarily because of the weather. The cold and the snow had made everything worse, and not just loading the ship. Roman had been driving the Lorry to and from the train stations for the Olim pickups. There are few plows in the mornings in Ukraine. You just did your best, following the tire impressions of other vehicles. Because we left so early, we were often the first ones on the road. Many times, when it was snowing heavily, we'd get stuck in a pit in the road or in a deep spot where the road was uneven.

When we were at the base, the heat never seemed to be enough, even when it worked. The hot water, when there was some, was at times only lukewarm, never completely removing the chill from our bones. The weather even made the food seem worse. We craved hot stews and hearty soups. Although the babushkas did make soup, it was mainly broth, with just a few pieces of meat and vegetables. I suppose it was sparse because it had to feed so many. At any rate, we were thankful that was now behind us. We looked forward to building ourselves back up over the next few days, as well as to spending time with the shipload of Olim, several of whom we would interview.

One married couple we spoke with was a retired dentist and doctor who were making Aliyah after forty-eight years of marriage. Again, how miraculous and faithful our God is to be able to, after a lifetime, open hearts to a move like this.

We also spoke with a seventy-five-year old holocaust survivor named Lydia. Her father had died in 1937. During the war the Nazis had confined her, along with her mother, sister, and brother, to a pig stable for seventeen days without food. Because Lydia looked more Russian than Jewish, the Nazi soldiers took her from her family and used her to sort the clothing and belongings of the Jews that had been executed. She eventually came across her own family's clothing. She said that Stephen Spielberg had interviewed her and that her testimony is on video in the Shoah Foundation in Jerusalem.

I took notes as the translator relayed Lydia's story. Each word that formed on the page was like the stroke of a deranged artist's brush. By the time Lydia was through, the eyes of my spirit could not view the picture that had been painted. It was just one more to add to the mural of sorrow and suffering that had developed during our fishing trips. Like a broken record, my heart echoed with the questions that had haunted me for the past four months: "How do these people survive? How do they do it?" I had seen and heard enough. It was definitely time to go home. I needed family and church, laughter, and fellowship. I needed light.

I held my tears, but my heart wept for this woman. We hugged and blessed her. Then we went back to our cabin to rest. And as the ship swayed, as it rocked back and forth, I strongly felt the Lord's presence.

His knowing hand gently guided my thoughts away from the darkness we were leaving behind and toward the joy of the time that was ahead of us.

The day we were to arrive in Haifa there was a farewell gathering with the Olim. We danced and sang many songs in Hebrew. The last was "Shalom Chaverim," which means "goodbye friends." The Olim hugged and kissed us, grasping our hands, their appreciation for all we'd done evident in their tears.

When we arrived, we were quickly processed through customs and then boarded a shuttle to Tel-Aviv. From there, we took a mini-bus to Jerusalem. It cost sixty-five dollars, which was a small fortune for us. We were on a very strict budget for the next two weeks. We had rented a room in Jerusalem, and we would have to pay for all of our food, except for lunch on the days when we'd be working for CFI (Christian Friends of Israel).

We didn't get to Jerusalem until eleven at night. After getting a bit lost, we finally found our room in a building on Jaffa Road. We had acclimated to Odessa, then the ship, and now here we were in yet another foreign culture. The money was different. The language was different. The thought of switching gears again made me just want to crawl into bed. But when Roman suggested we drop our bags and then go and visit Shannon and Billy at their hotel, it was as if I'd been given a shot of adrenalin.

I had forgotten how beautiful my daughter was. Four months had seemed like four years. As I held her, my tears wetting her peach-scented hair, I fully received this blessing. Our entire time away I had imagined, yearned for, the touch and smell of my children. Kissing Shannon over and over, in my spirit I witnessed the confirmation of God's faithfulness—"*I will care for your children, as you care for mine.*"

And not only had He cared for them, but also He had arranged for Shannon and Billy to be here in the Holy Land with us. It had been on Shannon's heart to visit Israel ever since we had gone on our tour the year before.

We spent the next day with Shannon and Billy and their tour group. We visited Jesus' tomb and the garden of Gethsemane, where Jesus prayed, "Father, if it is Your will, take this cup away from Me;

nevertheless not My will, but Yours, be done" (Luke 22:42). This was Roman's and my combined heart. We wanted, above all, the Lord's will for our lives. We were humbled to be walking in what we believed and had been shown in so many ways was His calling for us.

Our last visit with the group was to the Wailing Wall, where a year before Roman had asked the Lord to change his life. I remembered how afraid I was when Roman told me what he had prayed for. Now, not only had his life changed, but also through the work we had been called to do, the Lord had opened the eyes of our hearts in an irrevocable and unchangeable way.

Shannon and Billy left the next day. We had been so lifted by their visit, and we knew we would see them again in just two short weeks. As always, the Lord knew we needed that spiritual battery charge. We were about to confront something we never had expected in a land called "Holy."

Our volunteer work with the Christian Friends of Israel was, thankfully, not taxing at all. We worked only in the mornings at their distribution center, which received humanitarian aid from around the world. We were assigned to sort clothing by size into compartments for boys, girls, and adults. The time passed quickly. We spent the afternoons in the library sending emails to the kids and picking up a few small things to bring home. It was during these afternoons, as we immersed ourselves in yet another foreign culture, that I began to realize that even Israel, the land of our Lord, has its dark side.

I began to hear an edge in the speech of the Israelis, especially in that of the Orthodox Jews. A righteous pride stiffened their gait. It reminded me of that religious spirit we had experienced at the Messianic rally in Brooklyn the year before, when we were called "Jew killers" and I accidentally brushed up against a rabbi and he pushed me away in disgust.

I hadn't felt this as a tourist. But living in this culture as a Christian and obvious Westerner was totally different. When I shared this with another volunteer at the distribution center, I was told that others sensed this also. I hadn't expected to find religious oppression here. In many ways, these two weeks became as much of a battle as if we were back in Ukraine.

In spite of this, Roman and I had priceless times of solitude and reflection. We prayed and thanked the Lord for bringing us this far, for protecting and blessing us, for watching over our family. We continued to seek Him for our lives and for His purpose for us.

As we were leaving our flat for work on Thursday, December 17, 1998, our landlady told us that the U.S. had bombed Iraq overnight. She suggested that we avoid the open air markets when walking to work, because they had been used by terrorists in suicide bombings the past month. We also were told to be aware of packages left unattended in public places. For the first time, I became frightened.

From that moment on, we were alert and cautious. We knew that in Israel, anything could happen at any moment. As much as I knew that the Lord had brought us this far and had felt His protection over us, this new sense of fear made me even more anxious for home.

We had arranged to spend a few days with Shaul and Yael when our work with CFI was over. We had to take a bus to their house. Busses were favorite targets of suicide bombers. I sat in continual prayer in my seat, imagining what these people went through on any given day. In many ways, this was tougher than living in Ukraine. At least there you didn't fear for your life.

It was five days before Christmas, and I hadn't thought about it until we were on the bus. The holiday that we'd celebrated all of our married life, the most important Christian holiday, hadn't even crossed my mind until then. It was a reminder of how deeply we were into this work. The past four months had vacuumed all that had been familiar out of me. I felt isolated, disconnected, and hollow inside. All of a sudden, I began craving my family, my church, the decorations, the caroling, the lights, and the expectation of the season.

Shaul and Yael helped to fill the emptiness. It was good to be in their home again. While we were there, the last Ebenezer sailing for the year docked in Haifa. Shaul and Yael had invited the Ukrainian volunteers for dinner before we left the next day.

Having everyone around a table again reminded me of life on the base and of our times around the table in the babushka's house in Kirovograd. One of the Ukrainian volunteers told us that at a recent meeting with the Jewish people, a group of Neo Nazis walked in with a banner. On it was the Star of David with "Jews must be purged from Russia" on the inside. Anti-Semitism was on the rise all over the world, and all God wanted was everyone's heart.

As he had the last time, Shaul wrote a letter for airline security, telling them that we had been in his custody for the last two days. So we were waved through and boarded without incident. It was hard to believe that we were on the last leg of our journey.

When we purchased our tickets, they included a one-night stay in Vienna, where we had a seventeen-hour layover. Our hotel room was lovely. Like a child, I jumped on the queen-sized bed. The bathroom was brand new, fixtures gleaming. While Roman watched TV, I used every single one of the lotions and shampoos that sat on the marble sink top.

There was a full smorgasbord in the dining room—salads, fruit, pasta, chicken, beef, and fish. We had lived on falafels for the past two weeks in Israel, and we wanted to try every single thing that was there. They even had Christmas delicacies—small fruitcakes, macaroons, and sugar cookies decorated with evergreens and angels.

We turned in for the night exhausted and completely satiated. The next morning, we'd leave for New York. As I listened to Roman's rhythmic breathing and took in the sweet, clean scent of the pillow, visions of my children danced in my head. And beneath the down comforter, I clicked my heels, my heart repeating until I fell asleep, *There's no place like home. There's no place like home.*

Chapter 12 ✷

First Trip Home

And Abraham called the name of the place, The-Lord-Will-Provide, as
it is said to this day, "In the Mount of the Lord it shall be provided."
—Genesis 22:14

I HAD NEVER known such homesickness. I had never felt such a deep
love for my children as I did when returning from those four months.
Being away from them had necessitated severing a part of my heart. To
survive overseas, I had to strongly lean on the Lord and lay that part
of me aside for a time. But its sweet promise had always been there,
pulsating and beating with my very rhythms, waiting to be made whole
again. As the plane made its descent into John F. Kennedy airport,
Jeremiah's words roared louder than the engines: "I have loved you with
an everlasting love" (Jeremiah 31:3).

We were processed quickly through customs and retrieved our bags
with no problem. A friend from church, Bill, had offered to pick us up,
but when we entered the receiving area, he wasn't there. If it hadn't
been for all the standing, waiting, and bureaucracy we had endured
with the Olim, we would have been disappointed. Instead, we rejoiced
in being back in the States, found a bench, and began to breathe New
York back into our souls.

Within an hour, Bill rushed over to us, apologizing. It was just two days before Christmas, and the traffic on the Long Island Expressway had been heavier than usual.

Roman sat up front, filling Bill in on as much as possible in the hour and a half ride to Riverhead. Looking through the window of the back seat, I felt like we had landed in Oz. The sun shone brightly, mica glistening off the paved, litter-free parkway. All the cars seemed big, shiny, clean, and new, just like the leather-trimmed SUV we were riding in. Both sides of the highway were lined with shopping malls, their holiday decorations and lights beckoning checkbooks and credit cards.

I thought of our recent fishing trip, of Nena and Roza and their six and nine-dollar-a-month pensions. I thought of the family with the burned-out apartment and how all their earthly belongings would fit right on that backseat with me. Resentment began to rise in my spirit towards this land that I loved and had missed so desperately. I couldn't reconcile the everyday abundance of this country with the eternal need we'd left behind.

Before the car even came to a stop in the driveway, the boys flew out the front door. I pushed the car door open, wanting only to jump out and run into their arms. But as I tried, I was jerked back in, realizing I hadn't unbuckled my seatbelt.

My boys are both body builders, their embrace like a vise. In seconds, they hugged the months away, pressing every longing for them, every night of guilt and worry right out of me and into the frigid, December day. Roman, tears streaming, grabbed both his sons at once, wrapping his arms as far as he could around each one. It seemed he'd never let them go.

As I walked inside, a new appreciation for our modest home came over me. It seemed more open and spacious than I remembered. Everything was clean and in place. I knew Keith and Roman Eric had made sure that it would be. Thanksgiving took hold of me as I thought about heat, hot water, and a nice stove to cook on.

Shannon had left a Christmas tree on our front porch. She and Billy would be over later that day, and if we had the energy, we'd decorate it. But at that moment, the traveling, the reunion, and the cumulative effect of the previous months seemed to hit us all at once. We hugged the boys again and made our way upstairs to the bed we hadn't slept in for nearly four months.

Sleep was our main activity during the holiday weeks. Not having any thoughts of traveling, fishing, or sailing seemed to bring on an even greater need for rest, as if the Lord was telling us that this was our time to build up our reserves for what lay ahead. But our need for rest wasn't only physical. The last four months had drained us spiritually and emotionally. It was in these areas that our children opened the gas cap and began to refuel us.

They took over everything in the house, including Christmas. We hadn't had any money to buy presents for them, except for some bookmarks we picked up in Israel for their Bibles. We didn't care about exchanging gifts, but our children had brought us presents anyway. Shannon and Billy cooked a huge Christmas dinner. The boys kept the house and laundry up. But the most important thing for Roman and me was being around them. Having them so close, being able to reach out and hug them was the greatest present of all. I pressed my face into their hair and kissed their cheeks and necks. The aroma of my kids erased any memory of the stench in the flats overseas. I would come to draw on these moments, time and again, in the months ahead. In these short weeks at home, our children bore the fruits of our having centered our family in the Lord.

When we told the kids about our decision to return to Odessa in February, they weren't surprised. They said that from our emails they could tell we hadn't finished what the Lord had put on our hearts. Keith would be away at school this time, finishing up in May when we'd be returning. Roman Eric would be going back to school in Virginia. Shannon was newly married with a life of her own. The timing, which we knew was His, had worked out perfectly. And we knew our family would be okay, "for it was founded on the rock" (Matthew 7:25).

But after the holidays, after breaking the news to the kids, after having rested enough to handle it, we were blindsided by the reality of our situation. We were completely broke. We had a few dollars left in our checking account, but not enough for a major payment. The mortgage had been pre-paid for four months, but we were approaching the fifth month. We had each come home, literally, with just a dollar in our wallets. We had received some money from our church for Christmas, but that had already been spent on food and other necessities. If we were to get by, the Lord would have to make a way. And, as always, He did.

Shortly after the holidays, an electrician friend of Roman's offered him a temporary job at five hundred dollars a week. Almost simultaneously, one of the girls at my old job called, saying she was going on vacation for six weeks. She asked if I would fill in for her. This was how the Lord continued to work in our lives. No one came to the door offering us a million dollars, but He invariably orchestrated circumstances that met our immediate needs. Between the two jobs, we were able to pay, almost to the penny, the mortgage, the utilities, and our food. But we had no idea how He was going to provide for our return to Odessa. We'd need well over $5,000 to cover our airfare and expenses for three months.

As the weeks passed, we began to receive calls from different ministries. Apparently, word had gotten around, and we were asked to come and speak about our work overseas. We were anxious to share what we'd experienced, so were glad to accept.

We never asked for money. No one knew how strapped we were financially. But after these meetings, offerings were taken, and apparently people were extremely touched by what we had shared. At one church alone we were given a check for $2,500. At another, the offering was more than $500. This would more than cover our airfare to Odessa. What a testimony this was to the Lord's provision over our lives, and it was a faith builder for our kids.

Watching the Lord continue to provide for us like this only boosted our faith in and our commitment to Ebenezer's work. It was so obvious to us at this point that this was what the Lord had planned for that time in our lives. What a privilege and blessing it is to walk confidently in the will of Almighty God. It was truly as if we were walking on water, our hearts set like a flint on the One who maintained its spark.

We continued to trust God for the rest of the money we needed. But there was another obstacle we faced—trying to get multi-entry visas so that we wouldn't be restricted to entering and exiting Ukraine only once.

We went to the Ukrainian consulate in New York City, assuming we'd be able to get the visas the same day. But when we got there, a line of people was standing out in the freezing cold. This is what they did in Ukraine to humiliate you. I couldn't believe it was happening in New York. We waited in line for about twenty minutes before it started moving.

Once inside, we waited again. Just as it was our turn at the window, the frustrations we'd felt overseas began to rise. We were told that before we could get our visas, we had to leave our passports with them for a week and then come back with our airline tickets. We also were told that though we'd applied for multi-entry visas, there was no guarantee we'd get them. At this point, and with only two weeks until we left, we just trusted God

We hadn't fully unpacked when we got home, so that made our preparations for returning easier. And we now had a clear idea of what we needed and somewhat of an idea of what the weather would be like in February. Roman Eric and Keith had left to go to school, so we had already said our goodbyes to them. The only real issues for me were the loose ends in closing up the house. If I'd known that we were going to return to Odessa, I would have made a list of what I'd done four months earlier.

Though we were excited about returning, the prior four months had taken their toll. Since coming home, neither Roman nor I had been able to recapture the energy we'd had before leaving the last time. So the weekend before we left, we visited my mom (Detweiler) in Pennsylvania to draw from her bottomless well of faith and encouragement.

While we were there, my foster sister, Jean, was admitted to the hospital with lung cancer. We were told that she had only a few months to live. In light of this, we considered not going to Odessa and staying behind to see Jean as much as we could. But as we visited with her in the hospital, my mom there in the room, I felt a sense of peace. I felt that the Lord had His hand on Jean, that whatever happened, she would be okay.

Jean was a true believer. When she asked me if I had any words of wisdom for her, I told her the same thing I told my sister, Margie, a few years before—not to be afraid, and that I would see her on the other side of this life some day. My mom's strength through this was the anchor that steadied all of us.

On Monday morning we left Mom's and headed to the city to pick up our visas. During the ride, the thought of not seeing Jean again weighed heavily. There was so much in front of us that I couldn't afford to allow this to hold me back. So as I had done over and over in Ukraine when situations became unbearable, I prayed for the Lord to lift the weight. And shortly, though the reality of her disease still saddened me, I knew I'd be able to walk through it.

As we neared the city, I said a quick prayer for the Lord's favor to rest upon us. They did not issue multi-entry visas very often, unless you were someone special. We were nobodies. But we knew that the Bible is full of stories about nobodies on whom the favor of the Lord fell mightily.

Parking was impossible, so Roman stayed with the car, circling for a parking space, while I went in to the consulate. Once inside, I was called to a window by a young woman who had our passports in her hand. She leafed through a large stack of papers and asked me for my plane tickets. She looked them over carefully, asked me a few yes-and-no questions, then walked away toward a room in the back. I stood there waiting almost a half hour. Even though we were in the States, this was the Ukrainian government, modeled on the old ways of the former Soviet Union.

The young lady returned, animatedly conversing in Russian with a man I hadn't seen before. She was still holding our passports. Then he took them from her and went back into the room. Evidently there was a problem. But there was nothing I could do but stand there and wait and ask the Lord to intervene.

Holding our passports, the man finally emerged. He spoke with the young lady again, picked up and reviewed our plane tickets, made some notes, and then slid the passports through the opening in the small window. Without looking at the documents, I thanked both of the workers, tucked the small, blue books into my coat pocket, and went looking for Roman.

As I emerged from the building, he ran up to me with a big smile. He said that after circling the block a few times, someone had pulled out, and he had slipped into a parking space just a few doors down from the consulate. When he anxiously asked about the visas, I told him I hadn't looked at them yet.

As we got into the car, I reached into my pocket, praying that the Lord had been as favorable to us with our visas as He had been with the parking spot. I gave Roman his passport and then opened mine. I blinked several times before I was sure of what I was seeing. Not only had we been issued multi-entry visas, but also they were good for three years! We had applied for only three months.

I cried all the way home. God's care, protection, and direction over our lives had reached a new level, as if He were enabling us to "mount up with wings like eagles" (Isaiah 40:31).

We were scheduled to leave for Odessa on a Tuesday. The Saturday before, we were invited to share at a local church conference. In the foyer, along with many other ministries, we set up a small table covered with the Israeli flag and a few of Ebenezer's brochures. During the conference, one of the pastors asked Roman to share a twenty-minute testimony about our work overseas. He spoke beautifully, eloquently, and from the heart.

The next day, the pastor who had asked Roman to speak called and requested that we come to his office. He closed the door and motioned for us to sit down. Then he presented us with an envelope. He said there was a check inside that represented donations from Saturday's conference, as well as a missions offering from his church. As Roman slid the check out of the envelope, it may as well have been signed by God. It was not only the balance of what we'd need for our upcoming three months in Ukraine, but also it would cover our mortgage, which we had planned on borrowing from our credit cards to pay.

Through these circumstances and many others, God manifested Himself in our lives again and again, confirming the truth of His word: "Fear not, for I am with you; be not dismayed, for I am your God. I will strengthen you, yes I will help you, I will uphold you with my righteous right hand" (Isaiah 41:10). And like little children, we held tight to that hand as He led us once more across the ocean.

Chapter 13 ❧

Returning as Spiritual Leaders

Now therefore, go, and I will be with your mouth and teach you what you shall say.

—Exodus 4:12

THANKFULLY, WHEN WE arrived back at the base, they put us in "the hotel," the building where rooms had private baths. This was where all the base leaders were housed and where we had been fortunate enough to have been placed during our first term.

When we were settling in we were told that there was to be a meeting in the prayer room at eight. We had just arrived a few hours earlier. In our new capacity as spiritual leaders, we knew that part of our responsibility was to lead these meetings. The other aspects of our work would be explained to us in a separate meeting the next day. But we hadn't realized there would be a meeting that night, and we weren't prepared. Besides, we were completely worn out from traveling. But we had to go.

Roman opened the meeting with prayer and introduced himself to the new volunteers. They did the same, and then pre-arranged work schedules for the next day were given out. Thankfully, the meeting was a quick one, seemingly just so that everyone could have a quick introduction.

The next morning after breakfast we had our leadership meeting. There were six of us—three from Ukraine, a volunteer from South Africa, and Roman and me. As spiritual leaders, Roman and I were mainly responsible for heading up the meetings on the base. Roman would run the Tuesday, Thursday, and Friday night Shabbat meetings. I'd run the Monday, Wednesday, and Friday morning prayer meetings. The Ukrainian volunteers would fill in on our off days. Except for sailing days or to distribute work schedules, there were no meetings on weekends.

After the meeting we went back to our room. Roman's stomach had been upset since we arrived and hadn't gotten any better. He rested a bit as we talked about our new leadership duties. We had to carry these out in addition to everything else we would continue to be involved in—train pickups, handling luggage, fishing, and sailing. We felt like we could handle it, but it put a new perspective on our stay.

Before, we were part of the team of volunteers and had developed a comfortable camaraderie with them. Now we were more isolated, set apart from them. It was a bit alienating in that the base leaders didn't communicate and fellowship the same way the volunteers did. There was a strange sense of "power" that the leaders walked in. I think it was in part that hard, pre-war Russian mindset that they carried.

Over the next few days Roman got sicker and sicker with diarrhea. Everything he ate went right through him. I had brought some Pepto Bismol with me, but it didn't help. In all of it, he continued to drive the Lorry, transport the Olim, and manage the night meetings. But after seeing him double over in the bathroom one morning, I knew he'd have to see a doctor soon—although in that country it was a nightmarish thought. I prayed, anointed him with oil, and asked the Lord to please lift this illness from him. And, in the strangest way, He did.

One of the Australian volunteers introduced Roman to a solution called "colloidal silver." Two silver wires, attached to three nine-volt batteries, were put into a glass of water. The water then became electrically charged, and Roman was asked to drink it. The whole process looked like something out of the Stone Age, but it seemed to fit perfectly in our environment. Roman was willing to try anything at that point, so he drank it. And in the morning he felt much better.

With him on the mend, we plunged full force back into the work. We continued going to the train and bus stations in the early morning to pick up the Olim. The bases once again began filling up for the next sailing. Now that we had our multi-entry visas, we'd be going on most of the sailings. So the back-breaking work was balanced by the rest we looked forward to on the ship.

In our infrequent down times while at the base, Roman and I took walks to the Black sea, emptying our hearts and minds. We talked often about our visas and why we had been given them for three years. The more we talked about this, the more we felt the Lord beckoning us to stay longer.

The other leaders had shared that they had no new volunteers coming in on the next team who could serve as spiritual leaders. But we didn't know if a longer stay would even be possible. Our cash was limited as it was, and we didn't have much at home for the mortgage if we did stay. But at this point, with all He'd already done and in all the ways He'd already gone before us, we knew and trusted that the Lord would make it clear to us one way or another.

After our first week back, it was time to sail again. There would be 245 Olim on this sailing. We were now very familiar with the routine, although a bit put off by the deference the new volunteers were showing us. It wasn't bad in any way, just strange. I knew it was because we had become part of the leadership, but I didn't want to be viewed as an authoritarian. In my heart, I was a volunteer, just like they were.

Sailing day came, and there we were with the luggage—the loading, unloading, lifting, sliding, hoisting, and transporting the sea of bags. And there was the escalator again, unmoving, right beside us. Roman continued to be part of the team that handled the luggage, but in addition, he now had been given oversight responsibility, having to make sure all of the bags got properly delivered to the cabins.

I watched the now familiar but still difficult sight of Roman handling bag after bag. It was during this sailing that he injured himself for the first time. As the men were offloading the luggage from the buses, Roman was passed a particularly heavy bag that he grabbed in an unbalanced way. He said later that he felt excruciating pain as his right elbow snapped. One of the men saw what happened and immediately came over to pray with

Roman. After a few minutes, he was able to move his arm and fingers a bit, but his arm still hurt, and he couldn't use it. So he just did the best he could using his left arm as the other men helped him out.

As leaders, we were assigned deluxe cabins. Having never been on a ship before our previous sailing, I had no idea these types of rooms existed. We had a suite, with separate bedroom and living areas. The room included a sofa, a lounge chair, coffee, a coffee maker, cupboards with coffee cups, and a spacious bathroom that even had a tub.

As soon as we set sail, Roman took a steaming bath, soaking his arm in the hot water. Although the pain eased, we found out later that he had ruptured his bicep. And that arm has never been the same.

When it was my turn in the bathroom, I, too, took advantage of the luxury of a bathtub with a hot bubble bath. Sinking into the suds, I thought about the challenges we'd be facing this time around in Odessa. This was only our second week, but already we could tell how different it would be, not so much in the physical work itself, but in the underlying infrastructure that we'd had no exposure to before.

Even in this short time, we had formed a new appreciation for the leaders we'd been under during our first term. The administrative work involved in managing the relocation of hundreds of people was unbelievable. We were being made privy to all of it, assisting in pre-sailing checklists and documentation validations for the families. And then Roman had had to verify that every bag got to where it was supposed to go on the ship.

In addition, being spiritual leaders meant that we were the ones the volunteers would come to with problems and for prayer and spiritual support. We didn't have any blueprint to go by. This is where the nuts and bolts of this operation stretched, pulled, and pushed us. We weren't pastors and had little experience in counseling people. And to make things even more difficult, everything had to be spoken and translated in two languages. As leaders, we had no one except God to turn to when we ourselves needed support. Which, looking back, is exactly the way I believe He wanted it.

When we docked in Haifa, after all the Olim had disembarked, we got off the ship to make a quick call home. It was two in the morning, but this was one of the few opportunities we got to make an overseas call.

We called Shannon, knowing that she expected us to call at any hour of the day. There was something in her voice that concerned me, and I knew it had nothing to do with having just been woken up. I told her that she sounded as if something was wrong and asked if everything was all right. She hesitated, and then she told me that she was pregnant. Our first grandchild would arrive in November. I had to ask her to repeat herself, and she did. I put Roman on the phone quickly, just so he could hear it with his own ears. We screamed, shouted, and cried. My heart so wanted to be back home at that moment, to experience the fullness of holding my baby as hers grew within her.

Over the next month, in addition to the sailings and all that they entailed, Roman and I became more involved in other leadership responsibilities. We had to share the concerns and meet any special needs of the Olim. There were often changes in the status of the volunteers that we had to deal with—some needed days off, some got sick, some would leave. This would require reshuffling responsibilities and tasks. Also, prior to each sailing, we needed to organize fishing teams of volunteers who were staying behind until the next sailing. This was an enormous task that had to be shared among all the leaders. It required targeting areas for the fishing trips, finding homes/families for the volunteers to stay at during their trip, contacting all the families who would be fished for, and preparing all the parcels of humanitarian aid and all the brochures and flyers.

In addition, many times the fishing teams would visit churches and synagogues, so these had to be scouted out and contacted ahead of time as well. Before, we just went along and did as we were told. Now Roman and I were the ones doing the telling. All of this made us aware of and appreciate in a concrete way the mechanics that went on behind the scenes to make Ebenezer's organization run.

There were also visitors to the base, like Shaul had been, who were going on the sailings. We had to be aware of who these people were and where they came from and make sure that there were rooms for them. We also had to pick them up from the train or airport.

As we began to find our way through this new maze of responsibility, our dependence on the Lord became as natural as breathing. And looking back, I know that He stretched us in this way to force our dependence on Him. Our needs were far too great for ordinary people like us to manage. We were dealing with different nations, governments, and countries every day. We were sailing through foreign waters and speaking two different languages—sometimes three with Hebrew. We depended on God for the big as well as the small things. And when we became desperate for a worship leader, the Lord once again asked me to stretch myself.

I had learned how to play guitar many, many years before. I'd always loved music, and when I became a Christian, I couldn't get enough of praise and worship. We always needed a worship leader on the base and one on the ship. After the last group of volunteers had left and a new crew had come in, we found ourselves in desperate need for someone that could lead worship. No one on the team had come forward, and finally, one of the leaders asked if anyone knew how to play guitar.

There was an old guitar in the meeting room, leaning up against a wall. It seemed to have eyes that were staring straight at me. My heart began beating like a caged bird as I wrestled with speaking up. It had been such a long time since I played. But before I could talk myself out of it, my mouth opened and I said that I had some experience and would do what I could. The relief in the room was palpable, as worship was key to the spiritual strength of everyone on the base. Without it, I don't think the work would have survived.

I knew this responsibility would demand a lot of my time, particularly because I needed practice. Any time I had played in the past, it was along with others, never alone. In the days following, practicing the guitar became my first priority. Whenever I'd get frightened or felt that I'd gotten myself in over my head, I'd again call on Philippians 4:13: "I can do everything through him who gives me strength."

I continued to ask God to bring someone alongside me to help. Being in this alone, being in anything alone, was my weak spot. I suppose it came from my childhood and from the feeling of abandonment I'd experienced after my mother died, from being shuffled around from one foster home to another, one school to another. Ever since I'd met Roman, we'd been inseparable. But this was something he could not share with me. He'd be there, of course, in the same room. But he couldn't help in the way I needed him to. I simply had to trust God to send me someone. And after all He'd already done, it amazes me that I wasn't more confident that He would.

After I was well into the week, practicing and praying for help, one of the volunteers from the U.K. approached me and said that she loved to sing. She said it would be a privilege for her to sing alongside me as I played the guitar. Relief and thanksgiving flooded me as I silently apologized for my worry and concern. The Lord had come through, again and again.

I had heard stories from many missionaries about their lives abroad. Over and over they would share how the Lord provided for them in the most demanding situations. It was one thing to hear it, another to live it. I was reminded of the verse in Job where he says, "I have heard of You by the hearing of the ear, but now my eye sees You" (Job 42:5). I had always known that God is real, that He is interested in every aspect of us and our lives. But living that reality was doing something within us that would, in the end, be more valuable to Him and to us than the immediate work we were caught up in. He was changing, molding, and transforming our hearts. He was using this work to accomplish in us what nothing else had the capacity to do. And I wouldn't fully understand what that was until our work in Odessa was complete.

The volunteer from England turned out to be a perfect partner. We practiced for long periods, and when we were through, we felt like we wanted to keep going. I couldn't have picked a better person to stand alongside me. Her ease in worship was contagious, and I found myself just following her lead. It all flowed, as if someone else were playing the instrument. Roman told me that I played as if I had never laid the guitar down. He said there was always an anointing over the worship.

Over the rest of our time, we continued to sail, every trip a true miracle as the Lord brought more of His people home. And every Friday, whether we were on the ship or on the base, we shared communion. It was so necessary for us to come around the Lord's Table for healing, restoration, and the provision of so many needs. We all needed encouragement. Living was close. Frustrations mounted as weariness, loneliness, and homesickness set in. Our team represented many nations, each with its unique cultural orientation. Sometimes these would clash, creating friction among the volunteers.

As the spiritual leaders, Roman and I were responsible for trying to work any differences out, many times relying on the healing grace of laughter. We couldn't afford to have division among the team members. When Roman led the communion service, he'd share a word of repentance and forgiveness around the table, believing that the Word of the Lord would be received into those hearts that needed to repent, heal, and forgive.

Yet another responsibility we shared was to pay the staff on the different bases, where we had to deliver monies once a month. We'd usually use these opportunities to have lunch with the Olim, getting to know some of those who weren't living on our own base. During one of these lunches, Roman spotted one of the families we had fished for in Kirovograd. It was the family of four—father, mother, daughter, and granddaughter. He went over to their table, and they immediately remembered us. Those moments were what the work was all about— seeing the people we had fished for actually making Aliyah. We all continued to be humbled and stunned by how the Lord was using us to move upon hearts in such a profound way.

As the weeks went on, Easter came and went. The weather got warmer, more forgiving with each sailing—and they were nonstop. But the physical work, especially with the luggage, continued to pull and tax us. Combined with all the administrative and leadership work we now had, Roman and I found ourselves going in many different directions.

When the end of our three months came, we were asked by the leadership in Kiev if we would stay for another three months. There were no new spiritual leaders coming through on the next team. We had felt the tug to stay when we first arrived, and we knew that this request was the confirmation. The decision was not a hard one.

The kids took the news well, again saying they already knew we had been leaning in that direction. They encouraged us to stay as long as we felt we had to. I knew that the Lord had been faithful in preparing their hearts and that He would continue to be over them as long as we were in Ukraine.

We made arrangements for volunteers coming from the States to bring us additional funds. My foster sister, Jean, had gone to be with the Lord, and as He would have it, she had left me some money in her will. We were excited to be staying, encouraged and thankful that the Lord was continuing to use us in this work.

More and more, Roman and I got immersed in the administrative areas on the base. At the beginning of our next three-month assignment, an entirely new team of volunteers was brought in, and all the others left for home. We had to help these newcomers acclimate to the ways of the work. This included accompanying them to the train stations and to the other bases to show them the ropes there. Then on sailing day, we had to go with them to the ship to show them what needed to be done. Our days were full, our nights busy with Olim and leadership meetings.

Before one particular summer sailing, there was an incident we'll never forget. A family with a six-year-old girl named Natasha was staying on one of our other bases. Apparently the girl had been sick for a few days, and the doctor treating her diagnosed her as having brain cancer. He said she had a tumor that was aggressively making her sick and that she might not be able to make the trip to Haifa by ship. He also said flying her wouldn't be an option because of the air pressure. But if she could make it to Israel, where the medical help was sophisticated, she might have a chance to survive there. We quickly put out some international calls to Ebenezer's main office so that they could put out a prayer alert.

That night Roman shared a word to bring the volunteers together as one body. We prayed for this child and for the entire situation. We asked the Lord to keep her alive until we got to Haifa or else to take her home to be with Him before we left. We didn't want the child to die on board. The ship couldn't keep a corpse for any length of time. And if word got around on the ship that a little girl had died, it would cause all sorts of distress. There were only ten volunteers and over three hundred Olim. We wouldn't be able to manage comforting that number of people.

The day before we were to sail, Roman and I were asked to come and pray for Natasha, because she had taken a turn for the worse. When we entered her room, a small-framed, simply dressed young woman was carrying a basin to the bathroom. Her head hung and her countenance was dejected. I knew this had to be Natasha's mother and that she had probably been rubbing her down with cold rags.

The curtains in the room had been drawn to keep the heat out. In the darkness, the family's meager belongings seemed to disappear. There was a small bed in the corner, where Natasha's father was fast asleep. We tried our best not to rouse him, knowing that sleep was probably his best strength. In the middle of the room was a larger bed, where Natasha lay. She was curled up in a ball, her arms tucked inside. Her little body seemed to take up no room on the bed. Her tiny frame looked so helpless. My thoughts raced back home to the expert medical care we could give her. I was attacked by the frustration of not having the medical attention this girl so desperately needed. If she had been in the states or in Israel, she'd be on IVs, drugs, and monitors. But there she was, just lying on a bed with nothing.

The nurse on staff at the base had come in to see us. Through tears, she said Natasha had been running a fever and that she hadn't gone to the bathroom in five days. Her abdomen was hard as a rock.

Natasha's mother returned from the bathroom with a fresh basin of water. She put it down and picked up a New Testament. She was a believer and spoke English. As she talked, her soft cries and desperate heart pierced ours. We embraced her, blessed her, and then joined hands to pray. Roman prayed in English, covering the whole family with the Lord's grace and love. There was nothing else we could do but put this situation in God's hands.

We returned to the base, our hearts heavy. But we had to carry on with our work. The ship was sailing the next day. The night meeting still had to take place. Assignments for the ship had to be made. Luggage had to be packed and tagged. Sandwiches needed to be made, emails sent, paperwork and manifests completed. And amazingly, it all got done, the Lord's grace over us like a canopy. He had so cushioned our hearts that our minds were clear to make every decision and arrangement. We were amazed at the life we were living, going from one situation to another without even catching our breath.

On sailing day we were at the port when one of the volunteers' phones rang with the news that Natasha had died that morning. I immediately went to find Roman. He was unloading a bus. I pulled him aside and directed him toward the pier, close to the water. When I told him, he just sat down in the middle of the pier and wept. Most of the time Roman was a calm man, his words measured. But in this situation, he had no words. I knew how much this unsettled him, because this was the day the family was to have made Aliyah.

Roman had such a love for these people. Because of his European roots and because he and his family had immigrated on a ship to the promised land of America, he felt a special connection with them. I knew that in his heart he was processing the reality of what he'd just been told along with what could have been for this family.

But we had come too far and seen too many times how God had intervened in the lives of His people to question what had happened. We believed the Lord knew that Natasha would never make it to Haifa by ship and that taking her home was His mercy.

As we loaded the ship, news of Natasha's death spread among the volunteers. During the next three days at sea, we kept the family in special prayer and encouraged and supported each other. By the time we reached Haifa, all had come to terms with what had happened and accepted the Lord's providence.

When we docked, Roman and I got off the ship as we usually did, planning on making some calls home. Inside the port building, two of our Ukrainian volunteers who had stayed in Israel from the previous sailing rushed over to us. In a panic, they said that there was a problem with the ship returning to Odessa. It was a ship we hadn't sailed on before, a smaller one. Right after we had docked, the crew went on strike. Apparently they hadn't been paid in several months and refused to leave Haifa.

More than a hundred Russian tourists were waiting to board the ship to return to Odessa. There were ten of us volunteers. Five of our Ukrainian volunteers were still on the ship and not allowed to disembark. None of us were allowed to get back on. In the midst of the chaos around us, we gathered together and prayed. We knew that the Lord was in control.

We had to wait several hours in the port building before we were allowed to board the ship and gather our belongings. Since we didn't know how long the strike would last, our shipping representative decided that the most logical thing to do would be to get visas so that we could go to Tel-Aviv and fly back to Odessa.

As each of us handed over our passports to the police, the five western volunteers were given ninety-day visas. Our five Ukrainian teammates were denied theirs. For the first time during this ordeal, I was shaken. We had promised each other many times that we'd never be separated. All five had tears in their eyes, not knowing what would happen to them. We hugged them all, reinforcing that God was still in control, still with them. It was Friday evening, and Shabbat would be beginning in a few hours. Many agencies, bureaus, and airports would be closing down for a full twenty-four hours.

It was decided that the Ukrainians would return to the ship and the five westerners would remain in Israel. Our shipping representative had booked us hotel rooms in Haifa. As we exited the port building, three taxis immediately pulled up and practically ordered us into the cars. I was pulled away from Roman so that we were in different cars. But he had my passport, which immediately got me scared. You don't want to be in a country like that without identification, even temporarily. I didn't know where the hotel was. The taxi driver didn't speak English. I didn't speak Israeli. I was completely powerless. But after about twenty minutes, the taxi pulled up to the hotel. Roman was in the lobby waiting for me.

Our rooms were actually very nice, way up on the fourteenth floor. We could see the port from the hotel, and the ship, docked with our other volunteers. We continued to make calls to Ebenezer's main headquarters in England. They were aware of our situation and still trying to work something out in terms of flights. But it was Saturday, which was Shabbat, so nothing would be done that day.

We used the time to relax. Roman and I took a short walk into town, enjoying the quietness Shabbat brings to Israel. We talked about Shannon's pregnancy, wondering what she looked like, then in her fifth month. Almost at the end of our second term by then, after six months, we were overwhelmed with missing our kids. We knew we had to take times like these, and needed them, to think only about our family. Sometimes in the rush of the work, there literally wasn't a chance. And we knew that this work, if you let it, could override everything, even your family.

In total, we were in Haifa three days before we got word about our tickets home. And God used that time to impress something valuable on my heart.

On our last day, the group of us had decided to take a bus and visit the Bahai Gardens, a beautiful arboretum in Haifa. In front of me on the bus line, standing slightly to my right, was a frail woman. She was probably in her late seventies or early eighties, white-haired, and fair-eyed. As she was looking through her purse for change, the faded line of numbers imprinted on the inside of her left forearm zeroed in on my heart like a heat-seeking missile. I gestured to Roman, who immediately put his arm around me. Weeping, I fell into his chest.

It wasn't as if we hadn't seen this before. Some of our Olim had been in concentration camps, and we had interviewed many Holocaust survivors. It had never been easy and was always very emotional. But that afternoon, standing on His holy ground, those numbers spoke the very promise of God: "I will bring back the captives of my people Israel; they shall build the waste cities and inhabit them" (Amos 9:14).

At that moment, I had to call on the Lord to lift the thoughts of the horror that had preceded the living, breathing promise of the precious woman before me. I knew the Lord didn't want us to be overwhelmed like this, but to press on and trust Him. We needed to trust Him not only with our lives, but also with the lives of His people, because only He is strong enough to carry them and their past. It was this lesson, seared into my spirit beneath the noonday Israeli sun, that carried me through our upcoming and final fishing trips.

Chapter 14 ❧

Deep Fishing

I will say to the north, "Give them up!" and to the South, "Do not keep them back! Bring my sons from afar and my daughters from the ends of the earth."

—Isaiah 43:6

EXCEPT FOR A two-hour delay at the Tel-Aviv airport, we flew into Odessa through Istanbul, Turkey, without incident. Our five Ukrainian volunteers made it back safely three weeks later, the strike finally resolved.

By now it was July of 1999. Our rooms were like ovens, the temperature hovering at about 100 degrees. Air-conditioning was non-existent. The electric continued to go out intermittently. The cement pool on the base had been filled up for the little children. As a result, for a time we had no water, not even to flush toilets. The hot, sticky weather made it almost impossible to breathe. I longed for home, for the ocean and the bay where I had been swimming all my life. I thirsted for a cold ice tea and the laughter of my kids and my friends at the shore.

Over the next two weeks, before our final fishing trips, we had back-to-back sailings. It seemed that with each one, the number of Olim increased and more was demanded of us. In addition to Roman's leading the meetings on the base, he also drove the Lorry back and forth to the train stations. I could see that the heat was wearing on him. I couldn't decide which was worse—snow and ice or this blazing heat. Our added responsibility as spiritual leaders and all that was required of us, both from the team and on the administrative end, was now compounded by the physical work. We didn't know what our limits were. We just believed that the Lord would give us what we needed.

Gustav Scheller, Ebenezer's founder, briefly came through the base that summer. He told us how important it was to him that we fish especially for Holocaust survivors. He told us to "find them and spare no expense in doing it." He had an earnest desire to restore and put right those things that never should have happened. It was as if he had turned over a special burden from his heart to ours, and we took it personally. On our fishing trip to Kiev, we were able to do just as Gustav asked.

Besides Roman and me, our fishing team included our translator (a young girl from Africa), our Ukrainian driver, and a male volunteer from England. The trip to Kiev took about eight hours. We again used fields and bushes for bathrooms, but by then it was no big deal.

We arrived in Kiev about eight at night. Our first contact was with a local pastor. Roman, our translator, and I were to stay at his home for the week. The other two men would stay in another flat.

The pastor's home was simple, his wife a delight. After they spoke with the translator, she told us the pastor's story. His father was also a pastor. In 1946, he was tortured by communists for his Christian beliefs. For many years, his father had prayed for his son to accept Jesus. But that had been difficult, as the son had spent many years in the Soviet military. Yet here was the son, a pastor for several years now.

After a good night's rest and a wonderful breakfast, we were off to the Holocaust Association. We were met by a man named Igor Kogan and another man coincidentally named Roman. They had arranged a meeting for later that afternoon for us to speak with a large group of holocaust survivors. Igor had been only three years old during the war, Roman about fifteen. The year before, Igor found out that his father was one of the 200,000 or more Jews who were massacred at Babi Yar in 1943. After a brief introductory meeting, they took us to this horrific landmark.

The grounds looked like a massive park, but it was actually a massive graveyard. As we walked, observing many large, stone pallets in the ground, Igor spoke of the hundreds of Jews buried underneath. He told us that at one time the area was nothing but a group of very deep ditches. During the war, the Germans brought the Jews there (including Igor's father), lined them up, and systematically shot them.

Roman (the other holocaust survivor) then shared his story. His mother and six-year-old sister were being directed down the road, along with many other Jews, toward the ditch area in Babi Yar. Because of his age, Roman was pulled away from his family to be separated with the men. In the confusion with hundreds of people, Roman was able to jump off the road and hide inside a large pipe. He stayed there until evening, hearing the shots that killed his family. When all was quiet, he returned to his home to hide.

Igor continued, explaining the details of the executions. He said the Jews were ordered to line up at the edge of the ditches. They were told to removed their clothes, glasses, watches, and shoes, and place them to the side. Then they were shot, their bodies falling into the ditches, which remained open. Later, the Germans brought hundreds of Russian and Jewish prisoners to Babi Yar. They were assigned to retrieve the bodies and place them in newer ditches that had been neatly prepared with boards laid out on the bottom. They then were given gravestones from a Jewish cemetery and ordered to place these on top of the bodies. Then gasoline was poured over everything. This was repeated over and over, layers of bodies, stones, and gasoline, until all the dead had been retrieved from the old ditches, all the new ones filled, all the bodies burned.

The translator tried to keep her emotions in check as she relayed the horror story. As we walked these hallowed grounds, her voice periodically broke, and she had to be quiet for a while, wipe her eyes, and then continue. We were sickened and horrified, yet completely captured by this living account of the world's worst genocide.

Igor said the prisoners knew that the Germans were going to kill them. One of them somehow managed to get hold of a key that fit the lock to their compound. One night, as the guards were drinking and not paying attention, the prisoners made their escape. Twenty survived to tell the story.

At the Holocaust Association with Igor Kogan

Kiev Fishing Team at Babi Yar with Igor Kogan and Roman

We approached the edge of what seemed like a cliff. As Igor continued with more history, I felt as if I heard screams coming from the earth itself.

In 1962 there had been a massive explosion at Babi Yar. Dirt, water, stones, and skeleton parts were hurled for miles. The explosion was so massive that the debris reached a nearby village, killing 225 people. He said there was never an explanation for that eruption, other than that the earth had spewed out a chamber of horrors it could no longer contain.

To this day, the Soviet government does not acknowledge that area of Kiev. In 1985, they built a huge telecommunications tower on the property, as if to say, "Nothing happened here."

After a brief, low-key lunch, it was time for our meeting with the survivors. Through the translator, Roman explained Ebenezer's ministry then shared the Scriptures. When Roman was finished, I shared my heart and thoughts with them. There were about twenty people, all listening intently. Afterward, we were swamped with questions. Our poor translator, exhausted by then, answered them all. We left pamphlets and brochures, encouraging everyone to contact Ebenezer's Kiev office.

It was mid-afternoon by this time, and it had been an extremely draining day. We headed back to the pastor's house, longing for a hot shower and bed. We, unfortunately, just had to settle for the latter. There was no water at all in the apartment that night.

The next day was Saturday, Shabbat. We took the day off and enjoyed a tour of Kiev. On Sunday, Roman shared at the pastor's church about Ebenezer's ministry. The congregation opened their hearts to the message of Aliyah. Afterward, the pastor encouraged anyone who was Jewish to come to the front of the church, where he distributed brochures and pamphlets. We were glad to see some come forward.

Our fishing officially began on Monday. During our time in Kiev, we had hoped to visit twenty-five families. But we got called back to the base two days early, so we wound up meeting around fifteen instead. Their living conditions were similar to those we'd seen on previous fishing trips. All were grateful for the food parcels. Some had been at the very end of their food supply, with nothing to eat until we arrived.

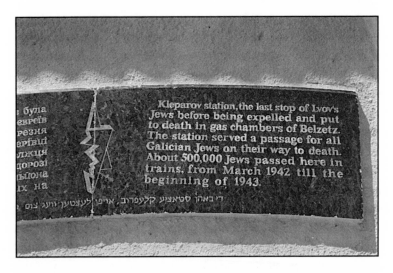

Memorial to Jews at Kleparov train station

Kiev holocaust survivor

Most of the people we met either had survived the holocaust or had family who had been killed in concentration camps. In one day, we met two different families who each had had eight family members killed by the Germans. We prayed with each family that the God of Israel would heal their wounds, which were beyond human power to heal.

So many of the survivors' stories read like movie scripts. All of them told of how they or their families had to hide from the Germans. They survived in the woods and ate off the land. They dug deep trenches and lived in holes in the ground, even in winter. One story in particular will haunt me forever.

On Wednesday of that week we visited a gracious, eighty-three-year-old lady. Her flat was much like the others, except it was very clean. You could tell she took pride in her home. Her story began in the early years of the war. One night, a few German soldiers came to her house. They had been drinking. They ordered her, her husband, and their two young children to get into their car, telling them they were going for a ride. The children were two and four years old.

They drove to a clearing in the woods and ordered the husband and two children out of the car. Her husband and one of the soldiers dug a deep hole. Then the Germans ordered her husband and two children into the hole. The soldiers then filled the hole with the dirt, burying her family alive. This woman was in the car, listening to the screams of her children. The soldiers then got back in the car and drove it over the mound of dirt again and again, until it was firmly packed down. Then they brought the woman to a camp. After the war, she returned to Ukraine and remarried. She never had any more children because she couldn't stand the sound of their cries.

"'Comfort, yes comfort My people!' says your God'" (Isaiah 40:1). But how could we possibly? This was the stuff of nightmares. I thought of my own children. And my mind hit a brick wall when I tried to imagine what this woman had endured, what so many of these people had endured. How did they do it?

We hugged this woman, prayed with her, and encouraged her about Israel. But like many of the elderly we visited in Kiev, she was hesitant to make the move, the trip, at her age. But some we visited, who were hesitant at first, seemed more open when we told them that we had taken

Team with woman whose children were buried alive

four generations home to Israel by ship. We left them the information and could do no more but pray.

We were asked to return to the base on Thursday, so we headed back. We drove through many farming communities, feeling like we were driving back in time. On the side of the road, people sold slaughtered pigs, their hooves protruding beneath coverings meant to keep the flies off.

The next two months were filled with train station pickups and sailings. On one September sailing, Roman was asked to stay behind because the base was short a driver. I was committed to the sailing as the worship leader, but the thought of being without Roman had never occurred to me. We hadn't left each other's side since we'd gotten to Ukraine. Now, for eight days, we'd be countries apart.

As I stood on the top deck waving goodbye to my husband, I felt just like an Olim. They always seemed to be leaving some family behind. For just a few moments, I felt what they felt. And I didn't like it. How hard this must have been for them. My only consolation was that the Lord's grace was over their lives and their family members' lives. He was their burden bearer. He had gone before them. He was bringing them home.

Without Roman, I leaned on the Lord even harder. Many nights as I rested alone in my cabin, I reflected over the work and our time there. We had given much more of our time and effort than we ever anticipated. What had started out as three months had turned into almost a year. This work had taken hold of us like nothing else ever had. It was the people that held us, the Olim, "the apple of His eye" (Deuteronomy 32:10). They had become stuck in our hearts and minds, the prophetic words of Jonathan Bernis two years earlier coming to pass in our lives. He had said, "May this burden for Israel stick to your spirits like glue." At this point, we almost couldn't pry ourselves away.

It had been almost eight months since I'd seen my kids. I hadn't seen Shannon pregnant. I had even considered not going home for the birth of our grandchild in November. I figured we'd be home in December, and we'd all be together then. This work was taking an unhealthy hold over my life, and I couldn't see it. But when I bounced the idea of not leaving until December off Roman, he was unyielding. Our daughter was having her first child. This baby was our first grandchild. We needed to be there with Shannon. Thank God for his clarity, his discernment.

Of course, he was right. The love for the work had slowly and steadily begun to compete with my responsibilities to my own family. My heart had become susceptible, and I was like prey for the enemy. Roman told me over and over that our children had to come before this ministry. It was as if the Holy Spirit had to shake me back to my senses.

I had never missed Roman so much as I did during those eight days. When we docked in Odessa, he was there at the port, waving a beautiful bouquet of flowers.

We were facing our last weeks before going home. We'd talked with the leadership about returning. They said they couldn't commit to anything at the time, but to pray about returning in May.

Our year had come to an end. We'd made many solid friendships with volunteers from around the world. We had taken thousands of Jewish people home to Israel. We had been part of an unprecedented move in history.

Chapter 15 ∿

Second Trip Home, Last Trip Back

At the command of the Lord, the children of Israel would journey, and at the command of the Lord, they would camp.
—Numbers 9:18

WE HAD BEEN home only two days when our granddaughter, Lauren, was born. We were both asleep on couches in the waiting room when a nurse woke us with the news. The baby was healthy in every way, and Shannon was doing well. We thanked God. We felt as if our lives had been rewarded by this gift of life. We wanted to do nothing but lavish our time in the upcoming months on our children and grandchild. But it was not to be.

Again, we had exhausted all of our finances. Roman had to work, and so did I. We thanked God for our electrician friend, who took Roman right back. I was able to return to work at the doctor's office.

When word got around that we were back, we began to get asked again to speak in several places. We knew the importance of sharing about this work, so we agreed to do as much speaking as we could. We spoke in churches, small gatherings, and fellowships. Many believers were touched by the first-hand stories we shared, and we knew that it was the Lord's timing. He wanted to open as many hearts as would allow Him. This work was far too great to lie dormant until we left again.

Sharing about our lives and work overseas wasn't an effort in any way. The work was embedded in our hearts, and we spoke what we had lived, the words flowing as easily as if we'd delivered speeches all of our lives. Between working and speaking engagements, we didn't have much time with the kids, especially with Lauren. It seemed as if the busyness of Odessa had followed us home.

When we thought about returning, it was as if we were discussing a dream. Once again, we had absolutely no finances and had to completely trust the Lord to provide. The situations we continually found ourselves in overseas had so stretched our faith that we didn't for a moment doubt that the Lord could do anything for us. If He truly wanted us to return in May, He would see to it that we did. We knew we wanted to return, but we couldn't open that door ourselves. We would have to be called back. We had to wait and see what God would do. We settled our hearts around this, determined not to manipulate the process in any way. I can't stress too strongly how miraculous this was for us. Our hearts had found a place in His work like nothing we had ever known. Yet, at the same time, we found such a rest in waiting on Him and for Him. It was like being on the mountaintop of faith, yet still living in the valley. It was truly supernatural living.

One morning in early February, we received a call from Kiev. The leadership asked us to return as soon as we could, if possible within two weeks. And they asked us to stay for ten months.

After hanging up the phone, Roman and I sat on the edge of our bed, our heads in our hands. This would put our faith over the edge like nothing else. Here were the "suddenlies" again, where the Lord can take your breath away. But we had learned that it is when all things seem impossible that, ninety percent of the time, the Lord is in the middle of it. We knew that if everything came together within two weeks, it would be the greatest display of the Lord's intervention we would probably ever experience on planet earth.

We estimated we would need at least $15,000 to pay our mortgage and bills for ten months, whether we were home or not. Our airline tickets would cost about $3,500 for the two of us. This was the bare minimum, not including expenses and personal needs. Our savings had been exhausted; there were no reserves to count on. We wondered how in the world the Lord would do this.

Over the next few days, the news spread that we had been called back to Odessa. On the heels of this, we were asked to speak at a private prayer group. There were only about eight people, all Jewish believers. We shared our stories about their fellow brothers and sisters in the former USSR and passed around pictures. We didn't ask for money; we never did when we spoke. But when we left, they handed us an envelope. As Roman drove home, I opened it. There in that envelope was $3,500.

Our church knew how committed we were to this work, and they completely supported us. Although they had blessed us with money before, we didn't realize how staunch their support was until the deacon visited our home. The boys were in the room when he handed us a check that, combined with the offering from the Jewish group, more than met our budget.

Our whole family was awestruck. Never before had we believed the Lord for this amount. I was sure this would increase my family's faith in the years ahead. I was certain they would never forget how their God provided thousands of dollars in a matter of days. When we realized that this type of intervention was on the same scale as that of thousands of Jews making Aliyah to Israel in spite of seemingly impossible circumstances, it all became very simple to understand. This was the God of Israel. This was His work. "Behold, I will do a new thing… Shall you not know it? I will even make a road in the wilderness and rivers in the desert" (Isaiah 43:19).

The biggest problem with leaving this time was that now we had a granddaughter. She'd be nearly a year old before we returned. She wouldn't know who we were. Having to separate from our family always pulled our heartstrings to the point of breaking. But we had to keep looking back at all that had supernaturally occurred for the encouragement to keep climbing that mountain of faith.

The day before we were scheduled to leave, I began experiencing unrelenting pain on the right side of my stomach. I called a doctor friend and explained the symptoms. He got me an appointment that same day. It turned out that I had a cyst on my ovary the size of a quarter. The doctor told me I shouldn't leave the country. He said I needed to be on medication for ten days to dissolve it and that in the process there could be serious side effects. But I trusted God with my whole heart, amazed at the place He had brought me to. Faced with this a year earlier, I wouldn't have had the faith or courage to leave. Now I had come to live in a whole new dimension, sensing the security of the Lord over my life. I had a peace in my heart, and I decided just to take the medicine and leave on schedule.

When my cyst dissolved without incident, I was reminded of the Lord's words through Jeremiah: "For I will restore health to you and heal you of your wounds" (Jeremiah 30:17).

Now so familiar with it, we got right back into the routine in Odessa.

During the first few weeks, we led the local fishing teams into the Odessa Oblast region. There were many holocaust survivors in that area. We sensed the mercy of the Lord calling them home in their final years. As we met each family, we heard the same stories over and over, much like in Kiev. Many had no relatives in Israel and wondered who would care for them. Many had lost spouses and held that responsibility toward the dead, feeling that they needed to continue to visit the graves. Most of them hadn't been to temple in years and were not familiar with the Scriptures. Most didn't even know or understand their traditions and holidays. To grasp hold of the freedom we were offering so late in their lives was nearly impossible for them. But we knew that the Lord had not forgotten them, which was why we were there. And as He always did, the Lord balanced these types of visits with the ones, albeit few, who received the message.

One visit was with an elderly lady who had already begun the process of securing her documents. She was overjoyed to see us, telling us that she had to stop the process when she ran out of money. We assured her that Ebenezer would pay the rest of the expenses. She cried, danced, and raised her hands to God. This was why we came to do this work. And this is how God reminded us not to get discouraged, that not everyone would respond, that it was all about the remnant. As Isaiah 10:21 says, "The remnant will return, the remnant of Jacob."

The ship we normally used for sailings, the *Dimitry Shostokovich*, wasn't available to us for our first and second sailings. It was only a month before the first scheduled sailing, and we still hadn't gotten word about a ship. This was obviously a huge issue, as Olim continued to pour onto the bases in expectation of the voyage to Haifa. Still, we continued with our work and continued to pray as a team, believing that the Lord would somehow provide a ship for us. And, of course, He did.

At last, we were told that Ebenezer had secured a Turkish ship, the *Iskenderun*. We would use this for two sailings. I could only imagine what this must look like to the Lord. Christian volunteers, a shipload of Jewish Olim, and a Muslim crew taking His people home to Israel.

I was beginning to worry about Roman. He continued in all he had done in the past, but weariness began to show. The work was nonstop and unforgiving. He was driving, loading and unloading bags, leading meetings, and overseeing other preparations for the ship. I didn't know how long either of us would be able to keep up the pace. But every time I thought about it, I had to force myself to stop and just keep going, keep trusting.

As Roman bore much of the physical work, I took on extra daily tasks at the office. These became a regular part of my everyday responsibilities. I was further trained in the financial aspects of the operation, such as paying the monthly bills. With each added responsibility, Roman and I were becoming more and more steeped in the work. And we were making real and lasting friendships with the Ukrainian volunteers.

By now, we were the seasoned volunteers on the base. The younger people looked to us for guidance and direction, both in the work and spiritually. With the extra responsibilities we were continually being given, Roman and I had to carefully measure how much we expended. When we could, we took our walks along the Black Sea. As we talked, we tried to flush any frustrations and difficulties into the vast, black water.

As the months passed, as the sailings increased, it became increasingly painful to watch Roman with those bags. All I could do was trust the Lord for him. And it was in these sailings, especially in the final months, that I realized we had taken on too much responsibility. When the ships were loaded, we needed rest. But as leaders, there was always something we had to do—attend a meeting, lead a meeting, interview Olim, do paperwork. Seeing Roman in these last months was what finally did it for me. Although he never showed his frustration and never pulled away from a responsibility, I knew my husband. And I began to feel in my heart that we were coming toward the end of our place in this work.

On one of our final sailings, we came across a new situation—a family who actually complained about their cabin. These people had lived in squalor most of their lives, so this was extremely surprising. It was a family of four, one of whom was an elderly, sickly woman. They didn't want her with them, and they also wanted a cabin with a window. We tried, late into the evening, to accommodate them, but we couldn't. The ship was full, and moving people around was out of the question. The family called us "fascists" and said they were fed up with our rules. I told Roman that the situation reminded me of what the Lord said to Moses about the Israelites during the first Exodus. Even though Moses was leading them to the land of milk and honey, just as we were, many in his charge murmured and complained. The Lord said in Exodus 32:9, "I have seen this people, and indeed it is a stiff-necked people!"

During our final months, we made two more fishing trips—one to Ivano-Frankivsk and one to Crimea.

Second Trip Home, Last Trip Back

Ivano-Frankivsk

The trip to Ivano-Frankivsk took fourteen hours. The van shuddered over pot-holed roads like a beast shaking off water. By the time we got to our destination, I felt like every one of my organs had shifted.

We stayed at the home of a pastor who was from Rock Church in Virginia. Again, we had no hot water during our two-week stay, and at times no water at all. The Lord had so stretched us by this point that the situation didn't surprise or stress us out as it had initially. I drew on my first fishing experience, remembering that I hadn't showered or washed my hair for ten days. I knew the Lord's grace would be over us on this trip as well.

Early in our trip, we met with one of our contacts. She was concerned about the evangelizing that some of the Christian ministries had brought to the area. Through our translator, we assured her that Ebenezer's goal is not evangelism, but solely to help the Jewish people return home to the land of Israel. She then committed to come alongside and help us. But she said that before she released the forty or so addresses of Jewish families in the area, we needed to meet with the local rabbi. We, of course, agreed, knowing that the success of this fishing trip depended on gaining the rabbi's trust.

The rabbi listened intently as Roman shared the Scriptures through the translator. As the rabbi heard for the first time the Lord's heart concerning his flock, as Jew and Gentile exchanged this understanding of God's purpose, I thought how miraculous it was. With each nod of the rabbi's head, God's Word was being manifested, "…so as to create in Himself one new man from the two, thus making peace and…putting to death the enmity" (Ephesians 2:15–16).

As our meeting came to a close, the rabbi not only made a call to our contact and gave her the okay to release the names and addresses, but also he told us about other villages in the surrounding area where many Jews lived. Once again, God's Word went forth and accomplished that for which it was sent (Isaiah 55:11).

One highlight of this trip was when Roman spoke to a group of holocaust survivors at a local synagogue. When we arrived, a group of about twenty-five people, all very elderly, greeted us warmly. They sat around tables set up in a large rectangle. Roman and the translator stood toward the front and shared information about Aliyah.

Some of the survivors wept, one woman uncontrollably. I went over to her with the translator and asked what was wrong. She said that two days ago she'd had a dream that someone was going to come to tell them about going to Israel. We hugged and reassured her "as one whom his mother comforts" (Isaiah 66:13). Our whole team was encouraged by this visit. The Lord had gone before us, preparing the hearts of His people to hear the message of return. He did, in fact, "... prepare the way for the people" (Isaiah 62:10).

After the meeting, the rabbi who had organized it took us on a tour of the town and shared its history. He drove us to a killing field, now a cemetery, where thousands of Jews were slaughtered during the war. The genocide of those days is beyond human comprehension. The rabbi showed us a monument that had been constructed in memory of the horrific persecution. Together, representing five countries, our team knelt at the base of the memorial. In our mother tongues, we prayed for the Lord's forgiveness on behalf of God's people. We prayed for the peace of Jerusalem (Psalm 122:6) and for the return of His people. We prayed for the rabbi and thanked God for the divine favor He had given us with this man.

Another highlight of this trip was when the pastor we were staying with asked Roman to share our message in his church. Through our translator, Roman shared the work of Ebenezer and gave a heartfelt sermon. He called the church to come to repentance for the atrocities perpetrated on the Jewish people in this area. I could tell that the parishioners were listening with their whole hearts. When Roman finished, he handed the church back to the pastor, who led the congregation in a prayer of repentance.

There were over a hundred people present at the service. Everyone, including our whole team, was on their knees. There were tears and cries of repentance. My Russian was getting better, and I heard people praying in Russian for their sins. Before this, I had never seen an entire church on its knees. It was truly a move of the Holy Spirit. Roman was humbled and grateful that the Lord had used him in such a tender, yet powerful way.

Roman speaking about Aliyah at Holocaust Association

Rabbi standing at monument in Ivano-Frankivsk

Crimea

Roman and I had looked forward to our fishing trip in Crimea. It is in the southern part of Ukraine, and we had heard that it was a picturesque vacation spot. The drive was scenic, the lush countryside proudly displaying its vibrant crops. But the geographic beauty of Crimea stood in stark contrast to the horrific experiences borne by its Jewish residents.

One woman we visited was named Yelena, a seventy-three-year-old holocaust survivor. Her nose looked as if it had been broken several times, and one of her eyes was not right. After the translator relayed some of her story, we understood why.

During the war, when she was eighteen, Yelena worked for an Austrian family. One day she was listening to the radio for news about the war when the Gestapo came in. After they heard what she was listening to, they beat her across the face, then put her in a truck and handcuffed her to another prisoner. They took her to camp Ravensbruck, the same camp Corrie ten Boom was taken to.

She told us about the lice among the female prisoners, the meals of broth and bread, and how the Germans, aware of the approaching Red Army, put prisoners on boats and then sank them in the river because of the atrocities they had witnessed.

As the translator relayed her story, Yelena cried and cried. I held her in my arms, and she laid her head on my shoulder. Again, here we were, living out the Lord's words through Isaiah: "As one whom his mother comforts, so I will comfort you" (Isaiah 66:13).

She told us about her eventual liberation from the camp and how the Russian soldiers called her a babushka when they found her. At eighteen years old, her hair had turned completely white. She was then taken to Siberia for another ten years of hard labor.

We washed her in the Scriptures for nearly two hours. We could see the cleansing begin as she said, "I have never met people like you before. You are like angels." We continued to love her, realizing that the

Me with Yelena

God of Israel, just as He said in Isaiah 30:26, was beginning to heal her wounds: "…the Lord binds up the bruise of His people and heals the stroke of their wound."

Yelena had no family, suffered from diabetes and other health problems, and felt that she should live out her life in Ukraine. We tried to encourage her to join a sailing and visit Israel, but felt that only the Lord could divinely give her this desire. We left her a food parcel and proceeded to our next family.

Michael, also a holocaust survivor, had difficulty walking, even with a cane. He was scheduled to make Aliyah with his family of eight on either the August or September sailing. This was wonderful news, but his story wasn't.

As a young Russian soldier, Michael was captured and sent to a camp with 15,000 other prisoners. No one knew he was a Jew because he had changed his name and said Christian prayers. All the Jews in the camp were forced to undress, and Michael was told to separate the good clothes from the bad. The adults were slaughtered with machine guns. They gassed the children.

Michael was eventually sent to Kharkov, where he had to walk forty kilometers a day. Those who couldn't walk were shot. There were hundreds of thousands of prisoners there, many, he said, driven to eat human flesh. He was one of the 4,000 who survived. He was eventually sent to Dachau, where he contracted tuberculosis. On April 29, 1945, the camp was liberated by the Americans. He became partially paralyzed after a mine exploded and badly injured his leg. After the war, he was hospitalized for nine years.

Though many did not survive, this man's miraculous story underscored the keeping power of God's Word over his life. Isaiah 43:2 says, "When you walk through the fire, you shall not be burned, nor shall the flame scorch you." And the fact that he and his family were making Aliyah! "Do not remember the former things, nor consider the things of old. Behold, I will do a new thing" (Isaiah 43:18–19).

Another visit we made was to the home of Roza. She was also a holocaust survivor, and her husband was Russian. They had never heard about Ebenezer or about Aliyah. Roza had a brother in Israel, but she hadn't seen or heard from him in over thirty-five years. Her husband was hesitant to go to Israel because he wasn't Jewish.

Roza's story was as heart-breaking as the others. Because of starvation, she had lost all her teeth in the camp when she was a young girl. When the camp was liberated, she weighed only forty-five pounds. Sixty of her relatives were killed in the camps. She told us that they constantly stepped over dead bodies and were forced to urinate and defecate on them. Her cousin had a baby in the camp, but it died within days because she had no breast milk.

Roza told us that near the end of the war, villagers would throw potatoes over the fence, and the prisoners would all grab for them. She told us that she still dreamt of reaching for a piece of bread but was never able to catch it in her hands.

As the people we visited relayed their stories, it was almost impossible for me to comprehend that these horrors had occurred within the century in which I was living. I had to make a conscious effort to turn my thoughts from the past and toward the work that all of us as Ebenezer volunteers were doing—following the call on our hearts to bring these people home. And in that, our faith was continually renewed as time and again we saw the Word of God come to pass. "Strengthen the weak hands, and make firm the feeble knees. Say to those who are fearful-hearted, 'Be strong, do not fear! Behold, your God will come with vengeance, with the recompense of God He will come and save you'" (Isaiah 35:3–4).

Before our final sailing, Roman and I had to meet with Ebenezer's leadership to discuss our future with the organization. A few months earlier, they had mentioned that they might want to open a new office in the Crimea area and would like us to run it. We felt privileged to have been asked, but it was an awesome responsibility. For one thing, it would require another year's stay. We would have to build the entire infrastructure, establish the agents throughout southern Ukraine, train the fishing and leadership teams, and manage the finances. We knew the energy we would have to expend was more than we could handle. We especially knew that now, as we were approaching the final weeks of our year there. We were tired to the bone, our minds and hearts truly spent. We knew the Lord, through this exhaustion that was of a different type than we'd yet felt, was telling us that it was time to go home.

When we met with the leadership, they told us that they had asked another couple to fill our current positions for the following year. They knew we were in need of a long rest. Although that was true, it was hard to hear that others would be taking our place. It wasn't an easy thing to let go of. We felt like after parenting this work for over two years, we had to give it up for adoption. They continued to ask us about the Crimea office, but we explained that we had discussed it and that it would be too much for us to handle.

After the meeting, Roman and I went back to our rooms, as confident as we could be about our decision. Going home, resting, and finally having a family life again seemed like the right thing to do. In our total time in Ukraine, we had seen 16,000 Olim return to Israel. With the grace and faithfulness of God, we had done what we had been called to do. Yet it was extremely difficult for us to lay this work aside. It had become our life, our very breath. The Lord's people had injected themselves into our hearts. As much as we wanted to go home, we knew it would be hard to leave. But we never in our wildest imaginations expected that it would turn out to be devastating.

Epilogue

I will not go, but I will depart to my own land and to my relatives.
—Numbers 10:30

AS I SAID in the beginning of this story, the mission field is a battlefield. But for the grace of God, Roman and I would have become casualties.

Upon our arrival, our house screamed of neglect. The lock on the back door had been jimmied and a few things stolen. We didn't have anything valuable really, except our privacy. Now that had been taken too. We shuffled through our musty home, each room pulsating with the absence of the joy and life our family had experienced there.

The ease of connecting with friends and family had been severed. We couldn't relate, not even to our children. We saw them, of course, but felt as if we had nothing to offer. Looking back, I see that all we did have had been given out overseas. Our love, energy, and support had been depleted, sucked dry by the searing need of the people, their stories, and the country. We tried to put on a countenance that our children could recognize. But they saw through it, and they became saddened and frustrated, knowing that there was nothing they could do.

I don't know why we thought it would be any different, but we came home absolutely destitute. While we had been in the work, our faith was at a zenith, and we didn't worry about a thing. The Lord had kept us going, sliding us into home base every time we were about to strike out. But now that we were back, the hope and promise that had sustained us for the past two and a half years were eerily gone. There were no calls to speak at churches. There were no visits, no monies being offered. It was as if without the work, we didn't exist—as if we'd left ourselves in Ukraine.

Roman and I had been transformed into the very Olim we had been called to minister to. I don't know how to describe it other than to say that we were foreigners in our own land, our own home, our own skin. We had become so other-absorbed that we couldn't relate to a society that seemed self-absorbed.

Roman worked for our electrician friend for a while. Then he landed a permanent job at a local hospital as a security guard—a far cry from the management position he'd given up before we went overseas. The job at the doctor's office was no longer available to me. I tried to find work, but doors kept closing. With our whole hearts we didn't want to, but we were forced to borrow money from Shannon to meet our mortgage.

For the first time in our lives, Roman and I felt vulnerable in our faith. After all our obedience, faithfulness, and sacrifice, we felt as if God had abandoned us. We never completely lost our faith, but the questions were insurmountable. We couldn't shake our feeling of isolation, of being misfits among our friends and neighbors.

We went to church, but it wasn't the same. No one really asked us much. They didn't understand that who we were before we left, who they had seen during our visits home, wasn't who we were anymore. It is so easy to mistake a person's outer demeanor for his or her inner one. As Scripture says, "…for man looks at the outward appearance, But the Lord looks at the heart" (1 Samuel 16:7). They didn't understand that we had been poured out overseas and were in dire need of replenishment.

Months went by. The feeling of being totally set apart never lifted. Roman and I started to have church at home, taking communion together. We prayed, many times with our faces to the floor, just as we had done years earlier when being called to the work. But this time we prayed for the Lord's mercy over our lives. In following the call that God had put on our hearts, we had lost so much, even the connection with our children. Our love for each other hadn't wavered, but the ease that love rested in had changed. In its place was a disarming discomfort and awkwardness, as if in some way we had to get to know each other all over again.

The months became years as Roman and I continued to try to adjust to our old life. But the adjustment never completely happened. We just learned, little by little, how to function again. We had to relearn basic things, like how to go to the store and buy food, how to talk to people, and how to socialize. It was as if we were being taken aside and placed in the wilderness of our own lives.

I often thought of how the Israelites wandered in the wilderness for forty years, when the trip could have been made in forty days. I thought of how Paul, after his conversion on the road to Damascus, had gone away for several years before starting his ministry. And of course, I thought of how before Jesus started His ministry, He spent forty days in the wilderness being tempted by the devil.

I talked about this with Roman, wondering whether we, too, were intentionally being set aside, being prepared for something. We didn't know, but as we had done our whole lives, we continued to trust the Lord. Because of what He had brought us through, because of all the miraculous ways He had protected and provided for us during our work overseas, we knew we had to keep pressing on in our faith.

For Roman, this transition and time seemed to be a bit easier. Although he was as devastated as I was about our circumstances, about the loss of the ministry work and the loss of our life as we knew it, he was able to carry on better than I was. I think much of it was due to his military training. He was a marine. He knew how to be strong. But I was experiencing the same rejection I'd experienced as a child. I felt unwanted, unneeded, and incapable of moving forward. I felt as abandoned by my heavenly Father as I had by my earthly one.

Then one day I heard God speak. It wasn't an audible voice. But I heard it in my heart, the same way I'd experienced revelations so many times overseas. What He told me was so foreign and so far out of my league that I panicked. What He told me was to write a book about our experience.

To me, the difficulty and seeming impossibility of this request far surpassed what He'd called us to do in Ukraine. That had seemed like such a natural progression in what we'd been involved with for years. But writing a book—especially one of the breadth required to describe what we had been through—was something I knew I couldn't do. I prayed and prayed, asking God to remove the weight of what He was calling me to do. Like Moses, when called to speak to Pharaoh on behalf of the Israelites, I argued with God: "Oh my Lord, I am not eloquent, neither before nor since You have spoken to Your servant; but I am slow of speech and slow of tongue" (Exodus 4:10). And as He said to Moses, so He said to me, "I will be with your mouth and teach you what you shall say" (Exodus 4:12).

So, for fifteen months I sat at my computer and wrote. Once I began, the words started to tumble out. I relived the details of our time in Ukraine—the emotions, the people, the places, the stories. At times my heart got so heavy that I had to walk away and try to remove myself from my own memory. It was in these times that I drew strongly on the Lord, on His Word and His promises, such as, "I will be with you. I will not leave you nor forsake you" (Joshua 1:5).

Four hundred and thirty-five pages later, I was finished. But I asked myself, "Now what?" I had been obedient and done what God had asked, but I was at a loss as to what to do with it. If God called me to write this, it had to be for a purpose. But I didn't know what that was, and with all my heart I had to trust Him for the help and direction that I would need.

I prayed over the book as if I were praying over the miracle of my very own child, because represented in those pages was the birth of a burden for God's people that was seared upon our hearts. And like that Faberge egg, the ancient call of Aliyah needed to be communicated with the utmost reverence, humility, and clarity. So again, like Moses, I asked God to send me *my* Aaron, someone who could help to bring about His purpose: "Oh my Lord, please send by the hand of whomever else You may send" (Exodus 4:13).

Nine months later, almost to the day that I had begun to pray over the book, God birthed yet another miracle. He sent the Aaron I had prayed for.

Through a fellowship lunch, a new member of our church found out that I had written a book and that I needed help. She was a writer, a new Christian who had been praying for a God-centered story. And she was a Jew whose ancestors hail from Ukraine. "Is not Aaron the Levite your brother? I know that he can speak well. And look, he is also coming out to meet you. When he sees you, he will be glad in his heart. Now you shall speak to him and put the words in his mouth. And I will be with your mouth and with his mouth, and I will teach you what you shall do" (Exodus 4:14–15).

Who could have arranged such a connection? Who could have answered prayers with such direction and intent, and through it, have forged a friendship anchored in His prophetic promises. I no longer need those anointed binoculars to see that it is the God of Israel. The God who parted the Red Sea to enable the first exodus is the same God who parted the Black Sea to enable our contribution to the second exodus. He is the same God who, through the miraculous, prophetic outworking of Aliyah in our day, is setting "His hand again the second time to recover the remnant of His people who are left" (Isaiah 11:11).

Amen.

Parting the Black Sea

From: EEF <eef@btinternet.com>
To: ebenezer@eef.intes.odessa.ua <ebenezer@eef.intes.odessa.ua>
Date: Friday, October 22, 1999 2:31 PM
Subject: Personal Message for Roman and Barbara Fialkowski

Dear Roman and Barbara

If I remember rightly, your time with Ebenezer is up, and I just wanted to send a message to convey my personal thanks for persevering in Odessa for a second season.

As members of the leadership team in Odessa, your steadfastness in the light of adversities brought stability and strength and your particular talents and experience, enriched and blessed the team. As leaders of the Western volunteer team, you invested your love, talents, time and tears in the lives of those who have served the Lord through Ebenezer. As you carried His people home, you poured out His love upon them. Your ministry to each of these was precious in His sight and you will be richly rewarded.

May the Lord continue to guide your steps in the days ahead, as you trust in Him. Thank you for laying down your lives to His glory. As you have served God's chosen people, no doubt rich blessings will follow you to the States.

"Therefore, my beloved brethren, be steadfast, immovable, always abounding in the work of the Lord, knowing that your labour is not in vain in the Lord" 1 Cor 15:58

Yours in Christ

Gustav Scheller
International Co-ordinator

Letter from Gustav

Ships we sailed on

Olim Statistical Information FSU 1999

Month	Date	Transit	Ukraine	Belarus	Moldov	Armen	Georg	Khisar	Novos	Mudus	Elelur	Kazak	Uzbek	Turkm	Kyrgiz	Tajiks	Total 1999	Total 1998
Jan	07.02-230		-	-	-	-	34	326	145	39	94	52	23	2	13		728	329
Febr	25.03-252		-	-	-	9	48	312	118	52	102	79	40	-	22		782	324
Mar	16.04-317	G-4	490	-	-	12	40	255	125	14	157	75	6	-	10		1184	571
April	06.05-279	G-1	313	-	-	12	26	370	155	24	140	70	78	-	7		1195	897
May	28.05-343	G-1	621	-	-	5	81	274	124	65	103	79	63	6	16		1437	759
June	14.06-313		591	56	-	14	69	308	199	61	160	126	53	12	13		1662	888
July	27.06-279	G-7	648	140	-	5	56	306	172	47	143	90	45	-	14		1668	1000
Aug	17.07-351		350	298	10	11	96	448	263	80	116	126	45	35	37		2025	1147
Sept	12.08-357	G-5 M-7	1032	267	40	13	66	384	428	77	234	111	36	15	9		2742	1325
Oct	02.09-330 10.09-361 25.09-353	G-13 M-20	991	181	19	18	107	431	385	83	262	14	25	9	19		2697	1528
Nov	04.10-333 18.10-354 25.10-337	M-13	1180	307	28	3	64	490	337	159	200	132	29	-	39		2959	1249
Dec	06.11-342 18.11-362 26.11-400	M-4	375	284		8	84	328	236	183	229	129	29	62	46	4	2025	1483
Total	04.12-379		6591	1533	97	110	771	4234	2707	884	2100	1215	472	141	245	4	21104	11500

G - from Georgia
M - from Moldova

Increase 9604

Olim statistics

Olim Statistical Information FSU 2000

Olim statistics

Breinigsville, PA USA
10 June 2010
239486BV00001B/4/P